THE JEWS OF
New Orleans
and the
Mississippi Delta

THE JEWS OF
New Orleans
⊷ and the ⊷
Mississippi Delta

A History of Life & Community Along the Bayou

Emily Ford & Barry Stiefel

H
THE
History
PRESS

Published by The History Press
Charleston, SC 29403
www.historypress.net

Front Cover Credits:

Top foreground: B'nai Israel Synagogue, Natchez, Mississippi. *William A. Rosenthall Judaica Collection, Special Collections, College of Charleston* (left); Phillip Sartorius and wife, Sophie. *Goldring-Woldenberg Institute of Southern Jewish Life* (center); Temple B'nai Israel, Baton Rouge, Louisiana. *William A. Rosenthall Judaica Collection, Special Collections, College of Charleston* (right).

Background: Map from John Foster Carr's *Guide to the United States for the Jewish Immigrant* (1912). *William A. Rosenthall Judaica Collection, Special Collections, College of Charleston* (top); Bird's-eye view of New Orleans, by John Bachmann published by A. Guerber & Co., 1851. *Library of Congress Prints and Photographs* (bottom).

Back Cover Credits:

Temple Sinai, New Orleans. *William A. Rosenthall Judaica Collection, Special Collections, College of Charleston* (top left); Touro Synagogue, New Orleans. *William A. Rosenthall Judaica Collection, Special Collections, College of Charleston* (top right); Leon Godchaux. From "Israelites of Louisiana: Their Religious, Civic, Charitable and Patriotic Life," 1904. *Louisiana Research Collection, Tulane University* (left).

First published 2012

ISBN 978.1.5402.3196.3
Library of Congress CIP data applied for.

Contents

Foreword

The New Orleans and Mississippi Delta region holds an important yet understated place in American Jewish history. This region, with the Mississippi River as its heart and New Orleans as its soul, stretches roughly from Vicksburg to New Orleans and includes many towns along the river that were once teeming with Jewish life. Many of the Jews who came to this region in the nineteenth century emigrated from Alsace-Lorraine and Central European lands; some arrived in New Orleans and then dispersed outward to the many towns along the delta. They frequently moved from one town to the next within the region, often marrying their Jewish neighbors, and many returned to New Orleans once they had accumulated wealth. These ever-expanding family and ethnic networks, which were shaped largely by the growth of the cotton industry, helped to carve out an economically and culturally unique region. The importance of the Jewish ethnic economy created within this region may be a model for the American Jewish experience more broadly.

There have been several studies of Jews within this region, but a comprehensive look at the interconnectedness within it, from the nineteenth century to the present day, is lacking. A few works have highlighted some connections within the region—the economic links demonstrated by Elliott Ashkenazi's *The Business of Jews in Louisiana,*

1840–1875 is perhaps the best example, while my own recent research attempts to unify the region by highlighting family networks and economic interconnectedness across state and regional boundaries. Other works chronicle family connections as well, demonstrating how marriage bonds and family networks united Jews across the area. Yet most scholarship on Jews in the delta is constrained by geographic boundaries and fails to integrate individual locations within their broader regional milieu. Some works, for example, focus primarily on either Mississippi or Louisiana, while others examine Vicksburg, Baton Rouge or Donaldsonville, among other places, but rarely does any scholarship fully transcend geographic boundaries. Even the region's urban center, New Orleans, lacks a comprehensive, analytic history that examines the city in relation to the region. While prominent scholars of American Jewish history have lucidly analyzed particular aspects and incidents within the region, their work, too, has not yet led to a synthetic and analytic regional history.

Drawing upon a wide variety of secondary works that cover themes such as culture, religion and economics, *The Jews of New Orleans and the Mississippi Delta: A History of Life and Community Along the Bayou* pushes us to think about this region in a more unified manner. It begins in the colonial period, covers the Alsatian and Central European migration in the early to mid-nineteenth century and describes the impact of the Civil War and Reconstruction on Jewish immigrants. It concludes by examining twentieth-century life, before contextualizing the region's history within the twenty-first-century landscape that we see today. Hopefully, this study renews interest among Jewish scholars in the interconnectedness of this important region, which will no doubt enrich our understanding of the economic, social and religious experiences of nineteenth-century American Jews.

—Michael Cohen
Tulane University

Acknowledgements

We would like to thank the innumerable representatives of Jewish historical and social organizations who provided material and insight for this book. Their knowledge and passion for preserving Jewish history in the small towns, big cities and entire region of Louisiana and Mississippi keep the story of these communities vital and alive. This work would not have been possible without them.

Our infinite thanks to Cathy Kahn of Touro Infirmary Archives in New Orleans. Not only does her knowledge of New Orleans's Jewish community know no bounds, but her great vitality, wit and willingness to provide guidance and images for this publication have been incredibly valuable. She is an inspiring woman and a joy to know.

Enough thanks cannot be given to Stuart Rockoff and Rachel Jarman Myers of the Goldring-Woldenburg Institute of Southern Jewish Life (ISJL). Their kind welcome at the ISJL's Jackson office, stimulating conversation and immeasurable knowledge of Jewish history in the South are without compare. Their involvement in this project has made it all the more enjoyable.

Additional thanks to the following for their contributions of images, advice and guidance: Joanna Sternberg, director of the Julius Freyhan Foundation; Sean Benjamin, public services librarian at Tulane University's Louisiana Research Collection; Irwin Lachoff, associate archivist at Xavier University of Louisiana; Dale Rosengarten, curator of the Jewish Heritage Collection at the College of Charleston Library's Special Collections; Michael Cohen, director of Jewish Studies at Tulane University; Lonnie Schaffer at Congregation Agudath Achim Anshe Sfard; the West Feliciana Historical Society in St. Francisville; the curators of the Historic New Orleans Collection; the staff of Harvard's Houghton Library; and Becky LeJeune at The History Press. We would also like to recognize the joint Clemson University/College of Charleston Graduate Program in Historic Preservation, as well as the College of Charleston's Urban Studies program for their generous support of us for this project.

Finally, special thanks to Donald Dura of New Orleans for his companionship, navigation skills, support and humor on the long and winding back roads between New Orleans and Vicksburg. Thank you for a wonderful experience!

Introduction

JEWS ON THE BAYOU

The Bayou Country, which includes New Orleans and the delta, is an area where the Mississippi River and Gulf of Mexico embrace in a green, watery ecosystem. Its cultural heritage is as rich as its dark, fertile soil. Indeed, there is a *mélange*, or mishmash, of peoples, languages and customs, from Cajuns and Creoles to southerners and Native Americans to African and European immigrants. Though small in number compared to other groups, as well as frequently overlooked, Jews have had a significant and long-lasting influence on this area. The colonial powers of France and Spain did not welcome them at first, however. It wasn't until Thomas Jefferson purchased the Louisiana Territory from France in 1803 that Jews could live freely on these shores. During the nineteenth century, a socioeconomic network of Jewish immigrant peddlers and shopkeepers from Alsace-Lorraine and Central Europe was established along the region's river systems, and New Orleans was at its center.

Bayou Jewry did not dwell simply, though; Jews were proactive citizens. They became philanthropists, pillars of industry, effective statesmen and defenders of their adopted home on the battlefield. At the same time, life in the "Big Easy" and the river towns north of the city was not always easy for Jews. They had to overcome anti-Semitism from various directions. However, the more endemic problem was the region's peaceful nature and the unquestioned acceptance of Jews in a seductive laissez-faire society. This resulted in a slippery slope in regard to assimilation,

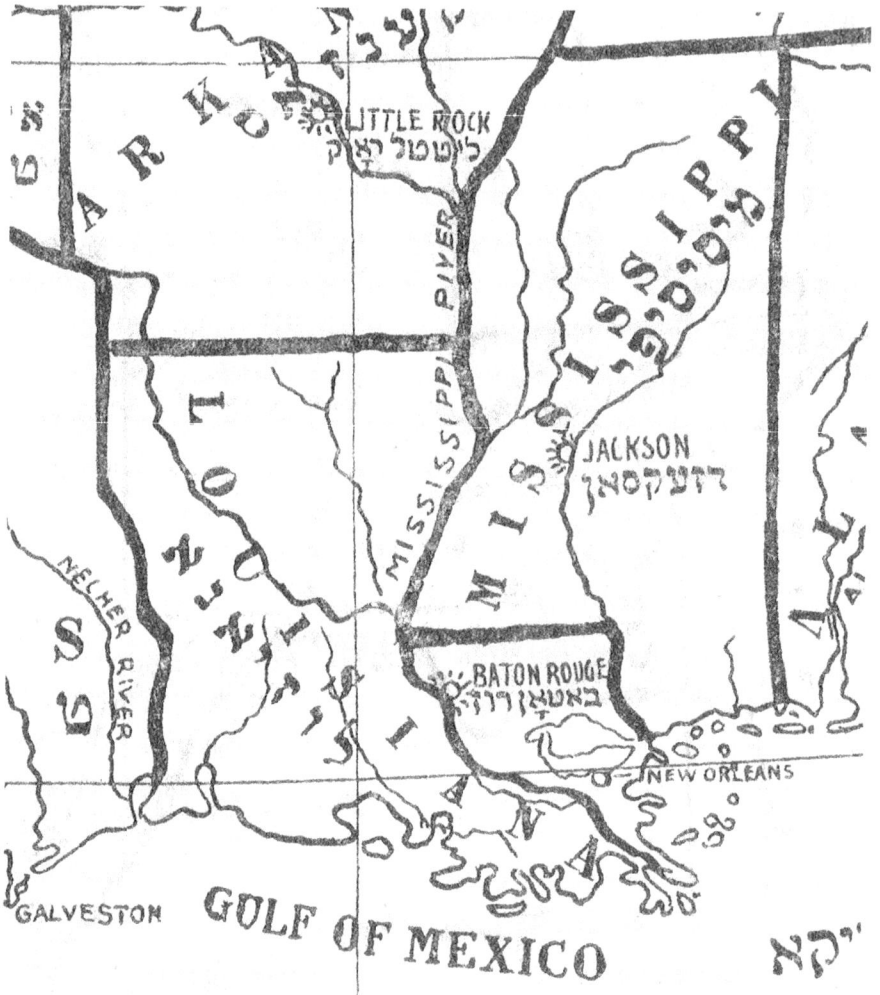

A map of Louisiana and Mississippi with English and Yiddish place names. Map from John Foster Carr's *Guide to the United States for the Jewish Immigrant* (1912). *William A. Rosenthall Judaica Collection, Special Collections, College of Charleston.*

especially when bayou Jews obtained economic and social success. How to be Jewish on the bayou became a difficult balancing act. Nevertheless, a Jewish way of life developed and flourished in its own special way.

Besides being contributors to the Bayou Country's culture, Jews were also influenced by the customs of Louisianan society, as well as the environment, and this allowed bayou Jews to create a unique and distinctive culture expressed in language, food, art and music. Jewish soul was maintained. After all, where else can one find such marvels as Mardi Gras' Krewe du Jieux and Krewe du Mishigas, the New Orleans Klezmer All-Stars, the Kosher Cajun Deli or a bowl of Creole matzo ball soup?

Judaism in the bayou region is by no means monolithic, and it is practiced in a variety of ways: Reform, Orthodox, Conservative, Chabad-Hasidic and agnostic. Sadly, since the late mid-twentieth century, the Jewish communities of the region—including those in New Orleans—have been in decline due to emigration and assimilation. The intention of this book is to encourage preservation of this heritage. Moreover, the best way to maintain a culture is be engaged with it and enjoy it. Thus, we encourage all who pick up this book to do so.

Shalom Y'all!

CHAPTER ONE

Louisiana and Mississippi in the Colonial Period

I n the mid-eighteenth century, the Mississippi River delta, which stretches from present-day New Orleans, Louisiana, to Vicksburg, Mississippi, was sparsely populated. Yet the people who came to the bayou were already diverse in origin, purpose and lifestyle. French traders scouted the wilderness for new settlements, while Spanish explorers moved eastward from New Spain in search of new colonial prospects. Meanwhile, Choctaw Indians, displaced by Europeans who were settling along the East Coast, had moved into the area around the mouth of the river. The region was poised for change, and no corner of the Mississippi River valley was more a crucible of that change than New Orleans.

The first documented Jewish settler arrived in this region, specifically in New Orleans, in 1757. Various land grants, newspapers, letters and legal records from this period serve as trace evidence of other Jewish persons who passed through the area. However, these indicators are based largely on assumption. The Caribbean world at this time was well populated with Jewish entrepreneurs who had planted roots in the tolerant Dutch colonies of Suriname and Curaçao, as well as British Jamaica and Barbados. These entrepreneurs often traveled from market to market, heading to wherever trade was most favorable at the time. In 1685, the French Crown issued a decree called the Code Noir, an edict that primarily regulated commercial and religious standards regarding

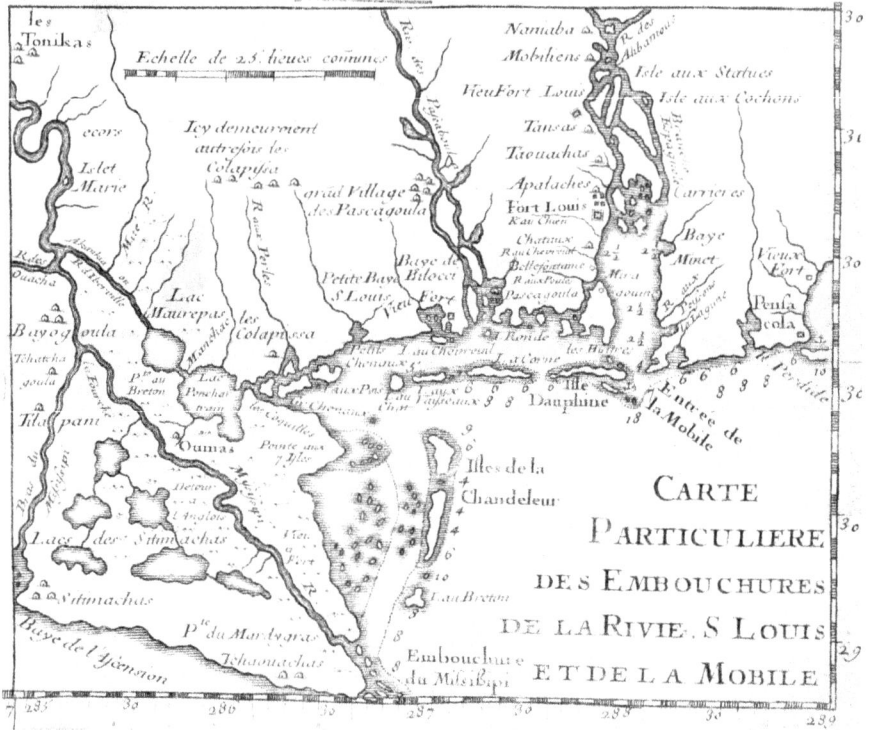

French Louisiana during the colonial period before the founding of New Orleans, circa 1718. *Library of Congress Geography and Map Division.*

the African slave trade. However, the edict's first three clauses included provisions for the exclusion of Jews and Protestants from all of France's American colonies, and that included Louisiana. The Code Noir was revised several times over the seventeenth and eighteenth centuries, although the most significant revision took place in 1724. Thus, while some Jews from the Caribbean and elsewhere may have traveled to Louisiana, their identity as Jews would have had to remain secret.

As the slave trade expanded in Louisiana, the question of the conversion of slaves was foremost in the mind of colonial administrators and missionaries. According to the Code Noir, slaves must be baptized as Roman Catholics, and the presence of non-Catholic slave owners threatened colonial leaders with the possibility of slaves becoming Protestants. Louisiana was also a proprietary colony, in which commerce was strictly controlled, and even religious policy was focused on maintaining that control. It is likely that the exclusion of non-Catholics from the territory was meant to remove commercial competition, be it from French Huguenot traders, Dutch Jewish merchants or British Anglican privateers.

While the Code Noir banned Jews in the colonies, it is widely accepted among scholars that the prohibition was preemptive, as no record exists of Jews who may have been active in Louisiana before 1724. Additionally, the colony was not prosperous enough at the time to draw much competition. It was not until later in the eighteenth century that economic factors shifted attention toward New Orleans. Even at that point, the French administration in Louisiana did not strictly enforce the regulations of the Code Noir, often turning a blind eye to the portion of the code pertaining to Jews. In fact, Isaac Monsanto became one of the most prosperous Jewish merchants in French New Orleans, often dealing with high-ranking figures like Chevalier Louis Billouart de Kerlerec, Louisiana's colonial governor.

Isaac Monsanto arrived in New Orleans in 1757 and quickly established a residence before gradually relocating his family to the city. His place in the mercantile economy of the New World is representative of the great network of trade forces present at the time. Having moved with his family as a young man from the Netherlands to Curaçao, he and his brothers engaged in transporting goods between French Saint-Domingue, British Jamaica, Spanish Cuba and the mainland colonies in North America. New Orleans factored heavily into his Caribbean business interests. In fact, it was in New Orleans's courts that Isaac and his business partners fought for restitution after British privateers seized a ship carrying cargo that belonged to him. This incident not only prompted Isaac to relocate to New Orleans, but it is also indicative of the city's burgeoning business landscape and the role Jews had in developing its trade relationships. By the time Isaac settled in Louisiana, he had already exchanged goods with coreligionists in Rhode Island and elsewhere. Isaac's brothers and sisters followed him to Louisiana soon afterward.

Isaac Monsanto and his siblings may have been the first to become established in New Orleans, but it is possible that other Jewish individuals and families of various origins moved to the city within the next decade. While Isaac developed his trade empire, correspondence between colonial officials suggests other Jewish businesses had developed in and around the city as well. By 1769, Louisiana had roughly 14,000 colonists, 3,500 of whom resided in New Orleans. Although the exact number of Jews who occupied the area during this period is not known, they definitely made up a small portion of the population, possibly fewer than one dozen people.

During the 1760s, France fought against Britain in the Seven Years' War, known in the New World as the French and Indian War. This war was waged on a large scale, which interfered with the bustling mercantile trade between the Americas and Europe. For the growing Crescent City, this meant obstruction of regular commerce, which forced the city into an economy of necessity. Jews and others who had engaged in Caribbean commerce with places like Curaçao, Jamaica and Saint-Domingue saw a growing market in New Orleans—seen as the gateway to the North American interior—and moved to meet demand. Motivated by the opportunity, other Sephardic Jews immigrated to Louisiana in the early 1760s. Isaac himself entered into the New Orleans scene with two partners, Manuel de Britto and Isaac Henriques Fastio, who had joined him from Curaçao. Other Jews who may have lived elsewhere but engaged in business in Louisiana were David Mendes France, Samuel Israel, Joseph Palacios and Alexander Solomons. While the Jewish population in New Orleans remained small throughout the 1760s, its members were significant figures in the colonial economy.

The Monsanto family—Isaac, his brothers Manuel, Benjamin and Jacob and his sisters Angélica, Eleanora and Gracia—was tightknit by any definition of the term. They often cohabitated in New Orleans, as well as in other residences they established over the years; numerous correspondences between the Monsantos show how affectionate and cooperative they were to each other despite the obstacles of distance and adversity. Isaac, considered the founder of the family's legacy, was by all accounts a shrewd businessman, often engaging in banking as well as his trading ventures. In 1766, he lived on Chartres Street in the present-day Vieux Carré (French Quarter) of New Orleans. Chartres Street would later become a Jewish business district in the early nineteenth century. In 1767, Isaac purchased a plantation known as Trianon outside the city limits. His success was widespread and shared by other members of his family. By the time the family was forced to leave Louisiana in 1769, Isaac Monsanto was among the city's wealthiest merchants.

The end of the French and Indian War caused a territorial shift that drastically altered the colonial landscape. The war had primarily been between France and Great Britain, but alliances between France and Spain had caused the Spanish to invest heavily in aid to France. With the close of the war and the Treaty of Paris in 1763, France relinquished its Louisiana colony to Spain, including the entire lower Mississippi territory. In turn, Spain, which had held territory in Florida and a long stretch of land along the Gulf Coast that extended into present-day Louisiana, ceded much of its holdings to Great Britain. All territory south of the thirty-first parallel remained in Spain's possession, and some of the holdings included the fort at Nogales, once known as the French Fort Saint-Pierre, and what would become Vicksburg, Mississippi. Thus, present-day Mississippi was divided between Spain and Great Britain, and Louisiana came under the Spanish crown.

Louisiana's transfer to Spanish control caused unease among the few Jews living in the territory, the Monsantos included. The local French colonial government's lax enforcement of the Code Noir had allowed these Jewish merchants and storekeepers to settle in the area, but the Spanish were much more restrictive in their economic and religious interests. The arrival of the second Spanish governor, Alejandro O'Reilly, brought the harsh reality of Spanish rule to Louisiana. Not long after his arrival, he expelled all Jews from the colony.

But O'Reilly's decree of expulsion was not limited to Jews; he banished all foreigners from Spanish Louisiana. This included all non-Catholics and even some French merchants in New Orleans. Jews were not welcomed in Spanish territory even before Spain's takeover of the colony. In 1492, Spain's King Ferdinand and Queen Isabella decreed that Jews were prohibited from Spain and its viceroyalties.

The fact that Isaac Monsanto was a Jew may not have been as relevant to the decree as was his fortune, property and overall success. Jews in

New Orleans and colonial outposts who weren't economic threats to the Spanish monopoly were left alone. Isaac Fastio, who had moved to the trade settlement of Point Coupee shortly after his arrival with the Monsantos in 1757, was permitted to remain, as were other less successful Jews. Marc Eliche, an Alsatian Jew, established a small trading post roughly fifty miles north of Baton Rouge in 1794 and operated it under the Spanish colonial presence without harassment. Regardless of the motivation for the expulsion, though, Isaac Monsanto was stripped of most of his property, including his plantation at Trianon, and made to leave with little remnants of his once great fortune.

The Monsanto family left New Orleans in 1769 and dispersed in search of stability. Manuel Monsanto may have traveled north within the colony toward Natchitoches, although he did not arrive there. Some sources speculate that he may have partnered with Isaac Monsanto's colleague, John Fitzpatrick, in the town of Manchac near Lake Pontchartrain in British territory. Benjamin and Jacob Monsanto also joined their brother in this venture. In the years following their expulsion and until Isaac's death in 1778, the Monsanto brothers frequently moved between the towns of Manchac and Point Coupee.

The undeniable resourcefulness of the Monsanto family is only one example of a greater trend among Jews who were involved in the Caribbean trade. These merchants had developed a culture of trade so wide and successful that historians have recognized it as an integral part of the economy of this period. Their commercial activities provided an indispensable source of American and European goods. Even in a hostile climate, the Monsanto brothers engaged in vital entrepreneurialism that foreshadowed the economic future of Jews in the Mississippi region.

The Monsanto sisters settled in Pensacola, then part of British West Florida. Over the next few years, all three sisters married non-Jewish men. Eleanora moved to Saint-Domingue, where she married Pierre André Tessier de Villauchamps. She would soon return to Louisiana and join her brother Manuel in 1775. Gracia married Thomas Topham and was also later reunited with her brothers. Angélica Monsanto married George Urquhart, an active leader in the West Florida colony, and the couple also moved to Manchac for a time before Urquhart's death in 1779.

Spanish forces captured Manchac during the American Revolution, and this disruption likely ended the Monsantos' activity in the town.

Isaac Monsanto died at Point Coupee in 1778 and never regained the wealth he had known while living in New Orleans, but he continued his entrepreneurial pursuits. Until his death, Isaac repeatedly visited New Orleans and other towns in Louisiana territory with little consequence. It seems that once the Monsanto family was eliminated as an economic power in New Orleans, the Spanish authorities had little interest in their presence.

After the death of her husband, Angélica returned to New Orleans to be near her brothers, who had moved back to the Crescent City and were continuing to manage the family business. She eventually married again, this time taking Dr. Robert Dow, a Protestant physician who was prominent in New Orleans philanthropic circles, as her husband. After marrying Dow, Angélica became a devout Protestant. She remained in New Orleans for the rest of her life, even when her new husband wished to escape the oppressive weather of the city and return to Europe. After she died in 1821, he returned to Scotland. Angélica was interred at New Orleans's Protestant Girod Street Cemetery.

Benjamin, Manuel and Jacob Monsanto continued to manage their mercantile firm and primarily dealt in land, commodities, dry goods, debt collection and slaves. Documentation shows that the three brothers and Isaac, before his death, made many small and a few large transactions in selling slaves, including a 1785 exchange in which Benjamin traded thirteen slaves for roughly three thousand pounds of indigo. Most merchants at that time engaged in slave trade as part of a wider range of interests. The Monsanto brothers did rather well in slave trading, as well as other areas. They purchased items that could be marketed in New Orleans and rural outposts, including liquor, clothes, silverware, lumber, fabric, tea, tobacco, soap, animal skins and horses.

By the 1780s and 1790s, Manuel and Jacob Monsanto had relocated to Toulouse Street in New Orleans. Benjamin, however, moved to Natchez with his wife, Clara, and their children and operated part of the family's affairs from there. He also established a plantation in Natchez by 1785. Then known as the Natchez District, the town was in the process of becoming a commercial hub. It was also strategically located on a high bluff on the eastern bank of the Mississippi River, and because other trade settlements like Manchac and Point Coupee had begun to decline, colonial powers fought over control of the district. By the time Benjamin Monsanto established his plantation along St. Catherine's Creek in Natchez, the town had become Spanish territory.

Although growing, Natchez was still small, with only about one thousand residents and very few merchants. Most early settlers in Natchez were, like Benjamin Monsanto, planters and farmers. Undoubtedly, the town proved to be an ideal market for the Monsanto brothers' partnership, and the townspeople held Benjamin in high esteem. His language skills in English, Spanish and French made him an asset in this transforming settlement. In an oft-quoted letter from Major Samuel Forman dated circa 1790, the major indicates that the Monsantos not only found it unnecessary to conceal their religion in the Spanish city but also enjoyed some personal notoriety in the town: "In the village of Natchez resided Monsieur and Madam Mansanteo [sic]—Spanish Jews, I think—who were the most kind and hospitable of people." Yet life as a planter did not seem to bring Benjamin much success. Evidence shows that his plantation venture was eating into his mercantile business shortly before his death.

By the 1790s, the Mississippi region was still a politically and socially volatile area. The early settlers found themselves sandwiched between the new United States and the Spanish Empire, which continued to dispute ownership of the territory, as well as vie for commercial use of the river system. Anticipation of opportunity and profit in the new American frontier spurred population shifts westward that would continue into the nineteenth century. The development of the Natchez Trace as a trade route spurred the growth of new towns along its path, including the settlement of Port Gibson. New Orleans continued to grow in population as well.

The manner through which the Monsantos and others expressed their Jewish heritage is difficult to ascertain. It is clear that while the Monsanto siblings were raised by practicing Jewish parents in the Netherlands, their assimilation into French and Spanish Louisiana societies left little freedom to engage in an established Jewish community. Even in private homes, there is no evidence of a Jewish congregation in the Mississippi region in the colonial period. Although life under French and Spanish rule had been relatively permissive regarding the religious backgrounds of its colonists, the practice of any religion outside the Roman Catholic Church was not well received in Louisiana. This social norm was so ensconced in colonial life in the area that Benjamin Monsanto likely had no other choice but to marry his wife, Clara, in St. Louis Cathedral, which he did in 1787. Indeed, marriage within a church was a common practice amongst crypto-Jews who resided in Spanish lands. However, with the exception of Angélica Monsanto Dow, none of these early pioneers converted. Converting to Catholicism would have prevented Isaac Monsanto's exile from the colony, but it is apparent that, although conversion was an option for members of the Monsanto family, no brother or sister was willing to deny their heritage. These Jews of the eighteenth century were part of a dynamic colonial world that rewarded adaptation and intuition. That they were secularists for the most part is not surprising, and their legacy carried on into the turn of the century, when many more like them arrived in the lower Mississippi River valley. To a greater extent, these non-practicing Jews and those who would soon follow were the norm rather than the exception. Overwhelming evidence suggests that, until the second quarter of the nineteenth century, "there were Jews in Louisiana, [but] there was no Judaism."

During the colonial period, New Orleans served as a gate city to an enormous frontier. It was also the principal port for all commerce along the Mississippi River and interior territories. Spanish rule had restricted aspects of trade occurring in the city but could not completely bridle the aspirations of merchants, planters, investors and even pirates. An elite Creole class had already developed in the city itself, and this class would guide political development within New Orleans over the next century. For the most part, members of this class were restless under the Spanish crown. The desires of this elite class, along with the desires of Napoleon Bonaparte, led to the return of French rule to the territory in 1800. This second French period hardly lasted three years, and the colonists themselves knew only by rumor that they were again under French rule. The territory was once again transferred in 1803, but this time, it would come under the control of the United States.

CHAPTER TWO

˿Antebellum ˿New Orleans and the Civil War

A t the time of the Louisiana Purchase, New Orleans was a rapidly growing city composed of numerous cultures and languages. Spanish rule had encouraged settlers from Mexico and Cuba to move into the area. French Acadians who had been expelled from British Canada migrated southward into Louisiana territory, where they would eventually become the ethnic group known as the Cajuns. Colonists from British West Florida also moved into New Orleans, as well as other towns that bordered the Mississippi River. Additionally, Native Americans from various tribes came to the city to trade. Migration from the United States westward accounted for a great deal of this population shift as well; many of the first Jews to arrive in New Orleans at the beginning of the nineteenth century had, in fact, been born as Americans. By 1800, New Orleans's population had increased to roughly ten thousand and would increase tenfold by 1860.

Joining the mostly Sephardic Jewish immigrants who had arrived in this early period were Central European Jews, many of whom were Bavarian and Alsatian. Some of these newcomers likely left Europe for personal reasons, but there were broader migration trends among Ashkenazic Jews already at work by 1803. In the wake of the Napoleonic Wars, the quality of life for Jews in Central Europe was miserably restrictive. Quotas were placed on the Jewish community regarding property, marriage and even

Bird's-eye view of New Orleans by John Bachmann. *Library of Congress Prints and Photographs.*

the number of children a Jewish family could have. The prospect of life in the new United States was attractive to many, and as letters came in from Ashkenazic Jews who had relocated to the New World, more and more individuals and families made the trip overseas. Over the course of the nineteenth century, the Jewish community in New Orleans would develop significantly.

The small group of Jews who were active in New Orleans in the first decade of the nineteenth century included both Americans and European-born men. They quickly developed professional relationships that transcended origin. The vast majority of them established businesses much along the same lines of Isaac Monsanto's, and this trend among Jews in New Orleans to engage in the retail, wholesale and general trade of goods continued for generations, although with many adaptations. Each individual engaged in his own aspect of this profession, often in partnership with other Jews in New Orleans and elsewhere.

Benjamin Spitzer and David Seixas were among the first American Jews to relocate to New Orleans from elsewhere in the United States, although their stay in the city was brief and not entirely successful. Coming from families who already had ties in New York, Philadelphia and Charleston, South Carolina, the pair established B.S. Spitzer and Company in 1804. The firm was located on St. Louis Street and primarily dealt in supplies that were brought into the city from upriver and abroad, including sugar, coffee and rum. Unfortunately, their venture did not enjoy prolonged success. The two declared bankruptcy and left the city before 1807.

However short a time Seixas and Spitzer spent in New Orleans, their legacy is important for a number of reasons. Primarily, their ties to the rest of the United States were indicative of a growing network of investment that would become the norm among Jewish businesses in New Orleans. Furthermore, Seixas had a particularly relevant investor backing his efforts in the city. Israel Kursheedt, a New York merchant whose family would also become involved with New Orleans's Jewish community, invested heavily in Seixas's ventures.

From 1803 to 1815, more than a dozen Jews entered the New Orleans economic and social landscape. Most concerned themselves with mercantile, shipping, retail and wholesale occupations, although some engaged in auctioneering and banking as well. Jacob Hart, who had lived in New York and Philadelphia, came to New Orleans sometime before 1805 and was involved with business concerns that focused mostly on the purchase and sale of goods from incoming ships. He ran a successful business for more than a decade, in part due to his own acumen but also with the aid of family in New York, who contributed capital and contacts. Furthermore, he entered New Orleans at a time of great economic activity; he may even have engaged in trade with the famous pirate Jean Lafitte, as many other New Orleans shipping agents did.

Hart's lifestyle in New Orleans was somewhat characteristic of successful merchants at the time. He owned a number of parcels of land and houses in and outside New Orleans, a cotton-press operation on Gravier Street, a number of slaves and partial interest in the trade vessel *Marsouin*. He also became co-owner of a plantation in St. Tammany Parish, which may have tied into his interests in sugar refining and cotton shipping. Jacob Hart was undoubtedly an ambitious man, and he enjoyed the profits of his ventures for nearly two decades before his luck soured. In 1823, Jacob Hart went bankrupt. Unlike Seixas and Spitzer, though, Hart's bankruptcy did not spur him to leave the city for greener pastures. His brothers joined him in New Orleans a few years after he arrived, and his sister and her family also relocated to the city in the 1840s. Jacob Hart established a true New Orleans family over the course of his lifetime, and his descendants became part of a greater Jewish community in later years.

Other intrepid pioneers in New Orleans during this time include Maurice Barnett, Alexander Hart, Salomon de Jonge, Asher Moses Nathan, Alexander Phillips, Ruben Levin Rochelle and Hart Moses Shiff. The business interaction between these men and other Jews in Louisiana at the time was extensive. De Jonge, who was born in the Netherlands and arrived in New Orleans by 1808, owned a business that involved the seizure and resale of property. In contemporary newspapers, he described his business as one of "commission and collection." His office was located on Condé Street in a building that belonged to Benjamin Spitzer and his partner, Israel Kursheedt. His business extended to Bayou Sara and Baton Rouge.

Maurice Barnett, Alexander Hart and Asher Moses Nathan also influenced the markets of greater Louisiana. While Hart and Nathan headquartered their firm in New Orleans between 1809 and 1810, the majority of their business took place in Baton Rouge. Barnett, who began his business in Baton Rouge in 1806 when it was still part of Spanish West Florida, moved to New Orleans by 1812 but maintained his professional relationships there. In 1831, he began an auctioneering company that he co-operated with his son, Maurice Jr. The company, which had its headquarters at the St. Louis Hotel on Royal and St. Louis Streets, traded in practically every commodity, including "furniture and other household equipment, ships, houses" and slaves. Barnett is historically seen as a slave trader, and while there were many in New Orleans, Barnett was particularly active. He advertised his business aggressively in newspapers and even had his name carved above his auction block at the hotel. He retired in 1850, and his sons continued the auctioneering company's other services long after the Civil War. Although Maurice Barnett died in 1865, his legacy lived on in a curious way; a picture of the Old Slave

Barnett's section of the Old Slave Block. *Detroit Publishing Company Collection, Library of Congress Prints and Photographs Division.*

Block on which he inscribed his name became the photograph used for postcards sold to tourists in the French Quarter. Today, this postcard is regarded as a curious memento of antebellum New Orleans.

Hart Moses Shiff and his partner, Ruben Levin Rochelle, were also active in New Orleans before 1815, and they were similarly colorful in what they accomplished. Described as a "peppery fellow," Rochelle was born in Hamburg, Germany, in 1780. Accounts describe him as a fiery businessman who published a furious note in a local paper after learning there were rumors going around that he was nearly bankrupt. Rochelle called those responsible for spreading the rumors "liar[s]," "scoundrel[s]" and "base" and declared, "The midnight robber is innocent when compared to him, who, under a mask stabs a man's character." Another newspaper article regales readers with a valorous tale, in which Rochelle, affronted by the crude behavior of city watchmen, scolded them for their offensive language. The officers reacted violently and later sought out Rochelle at his home. According to the article, the watchmen broke in, brandishing their swords, and "Mr. R" produced his sword in response and defended himself—a feat, the article reports, that would not have been championed "had Mr. R. been a weakly small man."

Hart Moses Schiff was born in Frankfurt, Germany, around 1780. Once in America, he dropped the "c" from his name, most likely in an attempt to better assimilate. Like all of the early Jews in New Orleans previously discussed, there is no evidence that Shiff was observant of his religion, and like many other non-practicing Jews, he married a French Catholic woman in 1813. He arrived in New Orleans sometime around 1810 and formed a business partnership with Ruben Rochelle. They enjoyed great success brokering shipments of commodities like tobacco, cotton and sugar that arrived in New Orleans's port. As was the case with most other Jewish merchants, they engaged in real estate, banking and insurance. The partnership of Shiff and Rochelle ended with Rochelle's death in 1824. Shiff died in 1851 in New York, although some of his children continued to live in New Orleans.

It is obvious that the earliest Jews in New Orleans shared a great many personal and professional characteristics. Most engaged in mercantile business, sale and resale of goods or the financing of such activities. There were, however, a few who did not fit this mold. Many of the children of these early Jewish merchants went on to become notaries. One man, Benjamin Levy, had established a printing business by 1811, which remained active at that location for nearly forty years and also had branches on Chartres and Conti Streets. The business, which included a newspaper called the *Price Current*, bookbinding services, wholesale and retail books and general printing, continued with Levy's son after Levy's death in 1860. Some of the immigrants to New Orleans also chose a different business path. Abel Dreyfous arrived in the city from Belfort, Alsace, in 1834. He eventually became a partner in a notary firm, and his archived notarial records document the transactions and official procedures of most of the Jewish businesses in New Orleans during the mid-nineteenth century. Manis Jacobs was a jeweler who arrived in New Orleans between 1809 and 1812 and would become instrumental in the development of the Jewish congregation Gates of Mercy in the 1830s. Undoubtedly, though, the most influential man in the development of New Orleans Jewish congregations was Judah Touro.

Although paintings and daguerreotypes of Touro depict him as elderly, he arrived in New Orleans at the age of twenty-five and was said to be a very shy and somewhat eccentric man. Touro was the son of a *chazzan*, or cantor, of Congregation Yeshuat Israel in Newport, Rhode Island, and according to records, his childhood was rocky. In 1780, when he was five, the Touro family fled to New York and later to Jamaica in 1782. The following year, his father, Isaac Touro, died, and his mother, Reyna, led the family to Boston to live with her brother Moses Michael Hays. In 1787, Reyna Touro also died, and their uncle raised Judah and his brother Abraham.

From his uncle, Judah Touro learned how to become a successful merchant. In 1801, two years before the Louisiana Purchase, he moved to New Orleans to open his own business. It is believed that Judah was one of the first Jews to permanently settle in Louisiana, where he became a broker and consigner of shipped cargo. Aspects of this profession became well established among Jewish businessmen by 1815, but Touro, given his presence in Spanish New Orleans fourteen years earlier, was possibly the first. He began to slowly accumulate his fortune by acting as a shipping agent and investing in shares of vessels himself. Unlike many merchants of his day, Touro conducted very little business in the slave trade. He is said to have even paid for the freedom of at least one former slave and acted as benefactor for another, although it is not certain whether this is true. As a consigner, he did manage the sale of innumerable other goods that came through the New Orleans port, including:

Linens, glass, brandy, soap, olive oil. Brandied fruits, almonds, wine, gunpowder, candles, beef, tongues, medicines, grass seeds, brimstone, paving stones, sulphur, lead, herring, furniture, dry goods, boards, mackerel, whale oil, codfish, rum, onions, cordage, cheeses, leather, salt…sugar, tobacco, cotton, skins, logwood, molasses, books, beeswax and calcutta goods.

It is said that Touro accumulated his wealth not by risk taking and unbridled ambition but by caution and asceticism. He never did become the most prosperous Jewish entrepreneur in New Orleans, nor did he engage in the elegant lifestyle that some of his coreligionists and colleagues did. He lived very frugally, perhaps as a result of his impoverished childhood, but the generosity he displayed during his lifetime marked him as a giant of philanthropy and stewardship to the New Orleans community as a whole and particularly the Jewish community, although this aspect of his benevolence really only manifested itself toward the end of his life.

Touro was an active member of New Orleans society between 1801 and 1815, but it appears that one great jarring event in his life caused this somewhat reclusive individual to withdraw from citizenship roles significantly. On New Year's Day 1815, Touro was seriously wounded while serving as an ammunition runner under Major General Andrew Jackson during the siege that would become known as the Battle of New Orleans. Research suggests that of the fifteen known Jews living in New Orleans at the time of the British attempt to capture the city, ten of these men served in American forces during the battle. They included Maurice Barnett, Jacob Hart, Samuel Kohn, Samuel Hermann, Ruben Rochelle, Hart Moses Shiff, Salomon de Jonge and Alexander Phillips. Many of these Jews were commended for their service in their obituaries. Maurice Barnett and another Jew named Isaac Phillips were both described in newspapers as lauded veterans who fought for their country, whether adopted or native.

Obviously, all of these men survived the ravages of the battle, as they went on to become figures in the New Orleans community. Judah Touro, however, suffered a gruesome wound to his thigh and would have been left for dead had it not been for his friend Rezin Shepherd, who courageously rescued Touro from the battlefield. Although Touro held Shepherd as his dear friend, confidant and executor for the rest of his life, Touro himself was never the same. He became withdrawn and was hesitant to make public appearances, and according to numerous correspondences from those who interacted with him, he was very slow when it came to making decisions. His contributions to social causes and, more specifically, the movement to develop a Jewish congregation would later mark him as one of the most important figures in Louisiana Jewish history.

Judah Touro (1775–1854). *Library of Congress Prints and Photographs.*

The religiosity of these early figures in New Orleans Jewish history is similar to that of the Monsanto family and, to some extent, the community that would develop in the city into the 1830s. Most married non-Jewish women and their children were baptized at St. Louis Cathedral. But like the Monsanto brothers, they never converted to Catholicism or any other religion. It seems as if religious activity within the French city was merely a matter of convenience. Even those Jews who married Protestants did so in the Catholic Church, and for these and others, documentation shows that services were held in a process customary for marriages of "mixed religion." As Jews, they were accepted into New Orleans society, but their heritage reflected their differences.

The early Jews of New Orleans were pioneers who were driven by the goal of establishing themselves and becoming prosperous. That they engaged in trade with other Jews in New York, Boston and Philadelphia suggests this Jewish identity expressed itself on a more social plane.

But more than anything, these first men were simply individualists. New Orleans was still a frontier town, and these Jews entered into the city's landscape alone from faraway places, effectively abandoning the communities that they were once part of. In the decades following 1815, New Orleans would see a gradual increase in the Jewish population, and most of these immigrants originated from Germany and Alsace-Lorraine. It would be these new arrivals, by virtue of their numbers, who would bring organized Judaism to New Orleans.

In general, immigrants and travelers would transform New Orleans in the 1820s and continue to do so throughout the antebellum period. The opening of territories around the Mississippi River to American expansion had brought about an agricultural economy focused on the river as a trade route. All manner of goods were moving into New Orleans. By the 1840s, New Orleans's population had swelled to 102,000 and was second only to New York in the number of immigrants it was receiving. Many of these newcomers would arrive in New Orleans only to continue on to other destinations. A number of Jews continued from the Crescent City to upriver destinations, including Port Gibson, Baton Rouge, Vicksburg and Natchez.

Jews from Alsace-Lorraine and Germany would compose the majority of the Jewish community in New Orleans for much of the nineteenth century. Like those who had left Germany at the start of the century, many wished to escape restrictive life in the Old World. The Jews who arrived as part of this migration and established lives in the city drastically altered the dynamics of the Jewish community from previous years.

By the 1840s, the community had solidified into definite neighborhoods, business districts and professions. The majority of Jewish businesses were centered on dry goods, groceries or clothing, and Jews were active in all levels of the market, including wholesale, retail and auctions. These businesses were heavily concentrated on Chartres Street. New arrivals from Europe would often begin their careers operating pushcarts along the river, selling their wares on the levees or as traveling peddlers. Often in the employ of a more established Jewish storekeeper in New Orleans or elsewhere, the peddler would take products on the road and travel across the South until he gained enough capital to open his own store. Over the course of the nineteenth century, the career of the Jewish peddler remained mostly the same.

Others arrived from New York; Charleston, South Carolina; France; the Caribbean islands; and elsewhere. Among those Jews present in New Orleans during the 1820s and 1830s were storekeepers and merchants, as well as dentists, carpenters, doctors, journalists and lawyers. There were also a number of proprietors of hotels, guesthouses and gambling institutions. New Orleans was a colorful Creole city full of the most skilled professionals and the most bizarre characters. Aaron Phillips, a Jewish actor who had performed in numerous cities in the East, performed at the St. Phillip Street Theater for a number of years in the early 1820s before returning to the dramatic circuit. Jacob Florance opened the Florance House Hotel near Lafayette Square in the burgeoning American Sector of the city and operated it until 1839. Another hotelier, Salomon Sacerdote of France, owned the stylish Frascati Hotel in the Clouet area of the city, which was considered a suburb at the time. Visiting families often went there to watch fireworks shows and balloon launches.

One of the most unusual Jews to live in New Orleans at any time was Daniel Warburg, a native of Hamburg who arrived in New Orleans by 1821. Warburg claimed to be a mathematical genius. His pamphlets on mathematical secrets to navigation and winning the lottery earned him fame, as well as a reputation for being somewhat unhinged. His mulatto sons, however, would become talented artisans. Not long after Warburg arrived in New Orleans, he began a relationship with a Cuban slave named Marie Rose. The couple had six children, two of whom gained local and widespread notoriety for their talents. Daniel Warburg Jr. became a stonecutter and engraver and was quite active in designing New Orleans cemetery monuments and mausoleums. Eugene Warburg was even more successful; he became a sculptor and moved to Europe, where he carved commission pieces for members of high society. He died in Rome in 1859.

Daniel Warburg was by no means the only Jewish man in Louisiana or Mississippi to consort and have children with a woman of color. Although interracial marriages were technically illegal, the practice of common-law marriage between white men and African, Native American or mixed-race women (known as *plaçage*) was common. Several Jewish men in colonial Louisiana had relationships with women of color (*placées*), and it is even thought that Judah Touro was one of them. This practice continued after Louisiana came under American control and was not restricted to the lower class; indeed, many of New Orleans's elite and well-to-do planters were involved with placées.

Although the Jewish population of New Orleans was growing, there is no evidence that congregations existed in the area before 1828. It seems also that no home in the area hosted Jewish services, and the expression of religion among Jews in the city had not manifested in such a way as to move toward that end. It is true that the Jewish community participated in its identity through social and professional venues, but the lack of a formal Jewish house of worship was conspicuous. It was more than obvious to Jacob Solis when he arrived in New Orleans in 1827, and he quickly set out to fill the void.

Jacob da Silva Solis, a member of a distinguished Sephardic family, came to New York from London in 1803. While he was not remarkably successful in his New York and Delaware ventures, Solis's story is one of caring for Jewish tradition in the New World. Sometime after Solis and his family moved to Mount Pleasant, New York, Solis taught himself *shechita* (the Jewish tradition of animal slaughter) in order to ensure that the meat served in his household was kosher. In the mid-1820s, he worked to promote the development of a Jewish children's academy. The school, however, never became a reality. After the lukewarm efficacy of his business ventures, Solis moved to New Orleans. He opened a store in 1827 and purchased some land with the hope of getting a share of the booming city's wealth.

If Solis was not the first Jew to be shocked at the city's lack of outward expression of Jewish tradition, he was certainly the first to take action in response to it. The story goes that Solis couldn't find any matzo to buy for Passover. No store carried the unleavened bread, and there was not a congregation in the city that he could ask to help him find it. Having no other option, Solis purchased meal and ground it himself. Not long after the holiday, armed with the same tenacity that had motivated him to become an informal *shochet*, Solis began a campaign to create New Orleans's first Jewish congregation. Described as "one of those determined, creative leaders upon whose shoulders the fate of the faith of Israel has always rested," Solis organized the establishment of Congregation Shaarei Chesed (sometimes spelled Shangarai Chasset and Shenarai-Chasset), or Gates of Mercy, and the congregation was formally established on December 20, 1827. The congregation was organized under the Sephardic rite, although more than one-third of its members were Ashkenazim from Germany, Alsace-Lorraine and Bohemia. It is possible Solis chose the Sephardic rite because he himself was Sephardic, but it may have also been a business decision on the part of the congregation's founders. Many of the established Jewish businessmen of New Orleans, the Atlantic seaboard and the Caribbean islands belonged to Sephardic congregations, and the founding members of Gates of Mercy may have adopted the Sephardic rites in hopes of gaining these individuals' financial support. They may have been particularly thinking of Judah Touro, who had already contributed to the support of Christian establishments like Christ Church. Touro did, in fact, donate to the foundation of Gates of Mercy, but he was not a member. In fact, many of the most successful Jews in New Orleans did not belong to the congregation, but many like Touro donated money to its establishment. It is also worth noting that at least eleven benefactors of the congregation were not Jewish.

Solis's ideals for the congregation had to be compromised in light of the somewhat assimilated state of the Jewish community in New Orleans at the time. In the Gates of Mercy constitution, accommodations were made for those members who had married "strange" (non-Jewish) women. According to Jewish tradition, the non-Jewish wife of a member of the congregation has to be converted if she too desires membership rights or to be buried in a Jewish cemetery. But in order for the congregation to be viable in the community, allowances had to be made. Approximately 50 percent of Jews in New Orleans had non-Jewish spouses. Even the congregation's first president, Manis Jacobs, had married a Catholic woman after his first Jewish wife died.

Solis moved back and forth from New York, where his family still lived, and New Orleans, where he worked. At the same time, he worked to organize the congregation and write its bylaws. Manis Jacobs, who would later be its first chazzan, was in constant correspondence with Solis, writing the store owner with questions regarding Sephardic tradition. In his letters, Solis guided Jacobs in rites of burial, marriage and other duties of the congregation. Even Jacobs, who consistently signed business documents with the name Menachem, his Hebrew name, likely had little skill in penning anything more in that language. Solis thus acted as the congregation's scribe. Interestingly, the congregation's bylaws were bilingual—written in English and French rather than Hebrew— and this reflected the congregation's desire to be an active participant in Louisiana's cultural environment. This is in stark contrast to Shearith Israel of Montreal, Quebec, the only other Jewish congregation located in Francophone North America at the time. With the British conquest of French Canada, the Jews who settled there after 1763 perceived themselves in Quebec society as strictly aligned with the English-speaking Protestant minority. This was, obviously, not the case for Jews in Louisiana.

Solis enjoined wealthy members of the New York and Philadelphia Jewish communities to contribute to the development of Gates of Mercy, as it appeared that many of the more wealthy New Orleans Jews were disinterested. Tragically, he died suddenly in New York in December 1829, leaving Gates of Mercy in its infancy and without a learned leader. Manis Jacobs was not trained to be a rabbi, but no other Jew involved with the congregation was either. Jacobs did, however, find a building in which to worship and perform weddings, funerals and Sabbath services. He purchased a plot of land at Jackson (now Jackson Avenue) and Saratoga Streets in 1828 for use as a cemetery, and the burial ground was used until 1847. As leader of the congregation, Jacobs made efforts to adhere to custom, although he confessed to Solis in 1828, "You know that I do not know much about the portugaise [Sephardic] minhag [rite]." Although his leadership in religious matters was unpolished, Jacobs is remembered for the advances he made for Gates of Mercy in the absence of its founder. After his death in 1839, he was given an honorary title of "rabbi" in his obituary.

The Jewish community continued to develop during the 1840s and 1850s. The Hebrew Benevolent Society, which held annual fundraising balls that were attended by people from all levels of New Orleans society, was organized in 1844. The Benevolent Society also formed an auxiliary called the Association for the Relief of Jewish Widows and Orphans and later partnered with the area's first Hebrew hospital, Touro Infirmary. Other benevolent societies were established during these decades, which was not only a result of the area's increase in the Jewish population but also a result of escalating public health issues. Historically, the environment was a breeding ground for pathogens like malaria, but the flux of bodies into New Orleans intensified epidemics with tragic results. The cholera epidemic of 1833, which affected the entire Mississippi River region, earned New Orleans a reputation as a "city of pestilence and death." Epidemics of "Yellow Jack" (yellow fever) ravaged the city nearly every year. The Jewish community was galvanized into action and quickly came to the aid of those who had become sick, widowed or orphaned by the plagues.

Three additional congregations were formed in the city in the 1840s and 1850s. The first, Nefuzoth Yehudah, or Dispersed of Judah, arose from a number of changes that occurred in the growing New Orleans Jewish community. In 1842, the Gates of Mercy congregation shifted services from the Sephardic to Ashkenazic rite. This change was likely due to the substantial number of Central European Ashkenazim who were relocating to New Orleans at the time, although it has already been established that the original congregation began with a substantial number of Ashkenazic members. Jewish culture was also beginning to spread and formalize in other parts of the country, in part due to the contributions and leadership of Isaac Leeser. Leeser was a chazzan from Philadelphia, but his activities in writing and publishing made him one of the most important Jewish men in the nation. He traveled throughout the country to help communities establish Jewish schools and, in the case of New Orleans, a new congregation. Leeser's advocate and agent in New Orleans was Gershom Kursheedt, the son of Israel Kursheedt, who was already connected with New Orleans's Jewish community. A professional editor and publisher, as well as a freemason, Kursheedt was the first treasurer of the Hebrew Benevolent Society and an observant Jew.

When Gates of Mercy moved away from the Sephardic tradition, Sephardic Jews, who were more established in New Orleans's society than other Jewish groups, were without a congregation. Furthermore, Gates of Mercy had gained a new leader after the death of Manis Jacobs—Albert "Roley" Marks. Manis Jacobs had not been thoroughly qualified to act as a spiritual leader of the congregation, but Marks was farcically inept. An actor by trade who often traveled with his troupe along the Mississippi River, Marks often complained that services at the synagogue lasted too long and even argued with the congregation during services. Letters written by area Jews note his character, suggesting that he was a man with the best intentions but he was clearly unqualified to lead the congregation during the 1840s. In fact, Marks may have inspired members to leave the congregation.

Gershom Kursheedt led the establishment of Dispersed of Judah congregation in 1845. The task of seeking out a house of worship led Kursheedt to Judah Touro. Touro at the time was a benefactor of several different institutions; not only did he donate money to Gates of Mercy,

Gershom Kursheedt (1817–1863). *Touro Infirmary Archive.*

but also he helped support Protestant churches in the area, as well as benevolent associations and some Jewish causes. Touro acquiesced to Kursheedt's requests and purchased the former Christ Church building, an imposing Greek Revival structure on the corner of Canal and Bourbon Streets, for use as a synagogue. A private ceremony was held on the morning of May 14, 1850, following the dedication of the building, and a commemorative stone was laid out in the synagogue. Ever the shy, hermetic man, Touro did not attend the public dedication ceremony that afternoon.

TERMS: from $1 to $5 per day; Slaves $1 per day.
IMPORTANT SURGICAL OPERATIONS CHARGED FOR EXTRA.

Advertisement for Touro Infirmary in 1852. *Touro Infirmary Archive.*

After the establishment of Dispersed of Judah, Touro became active in his faith for the first time in his adult life. In addition to attending services and observing the Sabbath, he purchased land on Gaiennie Street for the construction of a small hospital. Touro Infirmary originally only had thirty beds, most of which were occupied by the "indigent sick" and those served by the Hebrew Benevolent Association. The hospital was headed by Dr. Joseph Bensadon of Charleston, South Carolina. It was the second Jewish hospital in the United States, and it served all people regardless of creed. In the latter half of the century, it relocated to Prytania Street in the Uptown neighborhood of the city, where the institution expanded to become one of the best-known hospitals in New Orleans.

The infirmary was only one of a number of institutions that benefited from Touro's greatest gesture of benevolence: his last will and testament. He bequeathed thousands of dollars to dozens of religious and benevolent causes throughout the United States. Two of the synagogues that received his charitable donations were Dispersed of Judah, to which he left the synagogue at Canal and Bourbon Streets, and Gates of Mercy, to which he left $5,000. He also left sums of money to Touro Infirmary and other New Orleans benevolent societies, as well as to various Jewish and Christian organizations across the nation. One historian said of Touro, "We do not know of any previous American will, written by [a] Christian let alone by [a] Jew, which ever before had spread such largesse among so many institutions." It took the executors of his will, including his close friends Rezin Shepherd and Gershom Kersheedt, years to carry out all the bequests.

Judah Touro died in 1854, and his funeral services were carried out at Dispersed of Judah synagogue. James Gutheim, who had left Gates of Mercy the year before to lead Dispersed of Judah, officiated at Touro's funeral. His body was interred at the Jewish cemetery in Newport, Rhode Island. Isaac Leeser officiated at services for his reburial. The granite monument dedicated to him is inscribed with the following: "By righteousness and integrity he collected his wealth; in charity and for salvation dispensed it. The last of his name, he inscribed it in the book of philanthropy, to be remembered forever."

Both Gates of Mercy and Dispersed of Judah spent the 1850s solidifying themselves in the greater community. Gates of Mercy, which had been using an inadequate building on Rampart Street, built a new synagogue in 1851. The new structure had twin cupolas with delicate spires, ornate Corinthian columns and an arched parapet. In 1857, congregation Dispersed of Judah moved into a new synagogue farther uptown on Carondelet Street. The new building, also Greek Revival style, was designed by W.A. Ferret Jr. and was constructed by the firm Little & Middlemiss. Peter Middlemiss and Robert Little managed the firm, and both were prolific builders of residences in New Orleans's affluent Garden District. Their most renowned nonresidential buildings were St. Anna's Asylum and the St. Charles Hotel, both of which were built circa 1853. According to Middlemiss's obituary, he also built "Temple Sinai [in 1872] and nearly all the synagogues and a number of churches." Although there is no documentation as to who built the Gates of Mercy synagogue, it's likely that Little & Middlemiss did, as they had a reputation among New Orleans's Jews. Both congregations would continue to operate in their respective locations until the late nineteenth century, when they reunited to form Congregation Gates of Mercy of the Dispersed of Judah, also known as Touro Synagogue.

Surprisingly, an investigation of the 1860 census did not reveal any slaves in association with Peter Middlemiss or Robert Little's construction

Gates of Mercy synagogue on Rampart Street, built in 1851. This was the first purpose-built synagogue in Louisiana. *From* Israelites of Louisiana: Their Religious, Civic, Charitable and Patriotic Life, *1904. Louisiana Research Collection, Tulane University.*

Dispersed of Judah synagogue, designed by W.A. Ferret Jr. and built by the firm Little & Middlemiss in 1857. The two congregations merged to form Touro Synagogue in the nineteenth century. *From* Israelites of Louisiana: Their Religious, Civic, Charitable and Patriotic Life, *1904. Louisiana Research Collection, Tulane University.*

business, though further research is warranted if slaves by chance were being housed elsewhere. However, according to architectural historians S. Frederick Starr and Jan White Brantley, it was not profitable for builders of the Garden District to own slaves to use as labor for building trades during the antebellum period. Occasionally, builders would rent slaves for short periods of time or for specific projects, but low-wage Irish and German immigrant laborers were hired to help in the construction of the Garden District. The Garden District and the neighborhoods in the American Sector were where many of New Orleans's Jews resided and synagogues existed. It is quite possible that the South's two purpose-built synagogues in New Orleans were built without the use of slaves, unlike the synagogues built in Charleston, Montgomery and Savannah. Indeed, American landscape architect Frederick Law Olmsted observed on a visit to the city in 1853 that "the majority of the cartman, hackney coachmen, porters, railroad hands, public waiters, and common laborers…appear to be white men."

The second congregation to organize in the 1850s was located in an area that is now part of the Garden District but at the time was part of the Lafayette suburb of New Orleans. This area drew the most recent European immigrants, who operated businesses on the wharves along the river. The new German and Alsatian Jewish community there first developed their own benevolent society, the Jewish Benevolent Society of Lafayette, in 1849. By 1850, congregation Shaarei Tefiloh, or Gates of Prayer, had situated itself in a permanent building and had purchased a burial ground on Joseph Street. Gates of Prayer had a benefactor in its one-time president Abraham DeYoung, who contributed to the purchase of a building in 1855 for use as a synagogue. The little wood-frame building at the corner of St. Mary and Fulton Streets was dedicated by Reverend James Gutheim, the leader of Dispersed of Judah at the time, and was utilized by the congregation until 1866. While efforts were made to fund the construction of a new synagogue, yellow fever epidemics and the onset of the Civil War prevented its construction. In 1867, the new synagogue, located on Jackson Avenue near Chippewa Street, was finally opened.

The third and final congregation to be organized in the 1850s further reflects the diversity of origins and backgrounds that came together to form a Jewish community in antebellum New Orleans. Beginning in the 1850s, Jews from Eastern Europe, who would constitute the largest immigration wave to the city in the second half of the century, began arriving in New Orleans. The Polish and Prussian immigrants who formed congregation Tememe Derech, or The Right Way, were some of the first ethnic groups to emigrate from their homelands as a result of mounting anti-Semitism in Eastern Europe and pogroms in the Russian Empire. There would be a number of congregations formed by Eastern European Jewish immigrants in later years, but Tememe Derech was the only one to establish a house of worship in New Orleans. Its members met for worship and social functions at an adaptively reused building located on the 500 block of Carondelet Street until 1904, when the congregation merged with other, smaller Eastern European congregations to form Congregation Beth Israel. The new congregation purchased a mansion at 1616 Carondelet Street in 1905 and, in 1925, built a new synagogue at the same location. The establishment of Tememe Derech also marks the first development of a specifically Jewish neighborhood in New Orleans. By the 1870s, the "Dryades Street neighborhood" had become largely an Orthodox area, with a number of houses of worship, Jewish schools and kosher establishments. This neighborhood would have a significant impact on the larger Jewish community in the years to come.

The diversity of the congregations that developed during the two decades preceding the Civil War is indicative of what antebellum New Orleans society was like as a whole. A carnivalesque, beautiful, dangerous and squalid city, New Orleans was colorful, to say the least. There were substantial populations of Germans, Frenchmen, Irishmen, Creoles, Spaniards, Haitians, Cubans, free people of color, people of wealth and people of staggering poverty. The Jewish communities eking out their space in the Dryades neighborhood, on Chartres Street and in the synagogues on Rampart, Canal, Carondelet and Fulton Streets were not only another tile in the mosaic that became New Orleans culture but were also vital to the economic development of the city and the delta region as a whole.

This period saw the rise of the Jewish peddler. While some immigrant Jews before the 1830s made their living as country peddlers in rural

Mississippi and Louisiana, the sheer numbers of immigrants entering by way of New Orleans in the 1840s and 1850s predicated the growth of the profession. Many immigrants from Germany, Alsace-Lorraine and France began their careers in the New World through this avenue. Like the peddlers who operated carts along the New Orleans levees, the country peddlers would often partner with city storekeepers and wholesalers. Jews who were already established with stores or supply houses would provide the new peddler with products, and the peddler would travel through rural areas and sell their goods to plantations and small communities. Numerous permutations of this arrangement existed between country storekeepers and peddlers, wholesalers and retailers, factors and storekeepers and so on.

Economic relationships among Jews were paramount to the community; many newly arrived immigrants who were peddling in the antebellum period would progress to become wealthy retail operators after the war as a result of their associations with Jewish merchants. Leon Godchaux and Julius Weis, two men who rose to prominence in the New Orleans economy in the 1870s, were both doing business in the rural markets in the 1850s. Weis, who lived briefly in Fayette, Mississippi, would later become a storekeeper and cotton broker in New Orleans. Godchaux would become a wealthy plantation owner, the head of Godchaux Sugar Company and eventually the owner of a department store in New Orleans. Jewish identity, even in the 1860s, was still largely expressed through business and social interactions. Although the city's Jewish population in 1860 probably consisted of around four or five thousand people, it's possible that only 10 percent of this population was involved with a congregation.

Not every Jew in New Orleans was necessarily involved in some variety of retail, wholesale, auctioneering or peddling, although most seem to have been. Some of the first congregants at Gates of Prayer were painters, upholsterers, cigar makers, dockhands and architects. Gershom Kursheedt was primarily invested in the press and publishing. There were, of course, a few characters in antebellum New Orleans who were so different as to be avant-garde or even peculiar. "Roley" Marks was one such individual. But an even more unusual story in the Mississippi River delta's Jewish history is that of Adah Isaacs Menken.

Antebellum New Orleans and the Civil War

In late August 1857, Adah Isaacs Menken starred in numerous productions at the Gaiety Theater on Gravier Street in New Orleans. The New Orleans newspapers lauded her as a star, "an actress of real excellence…with her fine, natural abilities, her intensity, her clear, ringing, musical vocalization, and personal beauty." By the end of the Civil War, Menken would be one of the most controversial and mysterious figures in American theater to date. It is fairly certain that Menken herself was not born Jewish, but for all her allure, or possibly because of it, very little is certain about her background at all. It is clear that she was in Texas the year before she hit it big in New Orleans and while there, she married musician Alexander Isaacs Menken, a Jew from Cincinnati. She traveled with him as an actress throughout the South, but her debut at the Gaiety marked her rise to fame. Over the course of the next decade, she pushed boundaries of race, gender, art and polite society by not only performing male roles but also sensationalizing them. Her greatest role was as the Tartan prince Mazeppa in the play of the same name, a role that required scant clothing to simulate nudeness. She was a daring woman who smoked in public, and she was married six times over the course of her life. By the time she died, photographs of her were being sold at newsstands across the United States, marking her as one of the country's first true celebrities.

Adah's marriage to Alexander Menken was not long-lived; she claimed to be married to another man before she was even divorced from Menken. However, during her time in Cincinnati with his family, she not only converted to Judaism but also became involved in the budding Reform community there. She published articles that indicated her attachment to Jewish female figures, such as the prophetess Deborah. Rabbi Isaac Meyer Wise, a leader of the Reform movement in America, called her "our favorite and ingenious poetess." She continued to identify herself as a Jewish woman for the rest of her life. She died in Paris in 1867, but even in death, she remains a key figure in New Orleanean and southern Jewish history.

When Salomon de Rothschild visited New Orleans from Paris in 1861, he had much to say about the state of the city and of the American South as a whole:

Adah Isaacs Menken (1835–1868).
*Harvard Theatre Collection of the
Houghton Library.*

*New Orleans is a very French city which has preserved the customs of
the mother country…I asked what language I should speak in the city
and was told: "French on the right of Canal, English on the left"…we
are expecting the bombardment of Charlestown* [Charleston, South
Carolina]. *But what interest there is in seeing this new government
being formed! Men are enlisting en masse, but money is lacking.*

On April 20, 1861, de Rothschild wrote:

*What is astonishing here, or rather, what is not astonishing, is
the high position occupied by our coreligionists, or rather by those
who were born into the faith and who, having married Christian
women, and without converting, have forgotten the practices of their
fathers…And, what is odd, all these men have a Jewish heart and*

take an interest in me, because I represent the greatest Jewish house in the world.

In this letter, de Rothschild mentions Henry Hyams in particular. Hyams was lieutenant governor of Louisiana at the time the state seceded from the Union. Another Jew, Edwin Moise, Speaker of the House in Louisiana in 1861, appears to have taken interest in Salomon de Rothschild as well. Both men were ardent in their support of the Confederacy: Moise left his position as Speaker to become a Confederate judge, and Hyams remained lieutenant governor for the duration of the war. His sons all served as officers in the Confederate army, and his brother, Samuel Hyams, was a popular lieutenant colonel in the Third Division of Louisiana until his health forced him to retire in 1862. Numerous other Jewish men of New Orleans volunteered to serve the Confederate cause. Edwin Kursheedt, a nephew of Gershom Kursheedt, became a colonel in the Washington Artillery. Isadore Danziger, son of Theodore Danziger, an immigrant from France who owned a store on Canal Street, also served in the Confederate army as part of the Orleans Guard. The service of the Jewish sons and brothers of New Orleans was extensive. The most recognizable name in this list of Jewish Confederate men and politicians, however, is that of Judah P. Benjamin.

In his lifetime, Judah P. Benjamin would become one of the most respected minds of the Confederacy and a controversial figure blamed for some Confederate defeats. Born in 1811 in the Danish West Indies, Benjamin lived in Charleston, South Carolina, and attended (and eventually dropped out of) law school at Yale before the age of seventeen. He eventually relocated again, settling in New Orleans "with no other visible assets other than the wit, charm, omnivorous mind and boundless energy with which he would find his place in the sun." Over the course of the 1830s and 1840s, Benjamin became a lawyer in New Orleans and married Natalie St. Martin, a Catholic, in 1833. After achieving a certain amount of success, he built her a lavish plantation at Belle Chasse in present-day Plaquemines Parish, just outside of New Orleans. However, sixteen-year-old Natalie, who would remain distant from Benjamin most of their lives, was bored with plantation life and moved permanently to

Judah P. Benjamin (1811–1884).
Library of Congress Prints and Photographs.

Paris. Benjamin lived in the house until the early 1850s, when he was forced to sell it. The plantation was demolished in 1960.

Benjamin entered politics shortly after the sale of his plantation. He became a senator for the State of Louisiana, where he proved himself to be a skilled orator whose talents in logic and debate were admired among his peers. Benjamin, although not an observant Jew, did not deny his identity. He was also quick with words, and according to one story, Benjamin, in response to a political adversary's snide comments regarding his heritage, retorted, "It is true that I am a Jew, and when my ancestors were receiving the Ten Commandments from the immediate hand of Deity, midst the thunderings and lightnings of Mount Sinai, the ancestors of my opponent were herding swine in the forest of Great Britain."

By September 1861, Benjamin had become secretary of war for the Confederacy, a position that would earn him derision as well as praise. Even at this early point in the war, the dangerously ill-equipped state of the Confederate armed forces was obvious to Benjamin. Supplies were difficult to secure, and communications and infrastructure in the

South were inadequate. Confederate generals argued with him, and he generally found the cards stacked against him. Jefferson Davis appointed Benjamin as secretary of state in 1862, which was a less contentious office. He served in that position for the rest of the war.

After the surrender at Appomattox, Benjamin disguised himself and made his way to Florida and, from there, fled the country. He traveled to London afterward, where he reengineered his career as a lawyer. When his health began to fail, he moved in with his wife, Natalie, in Paris. It was the first time the couple had lived together in forty years. Upon Benjamin's death in 1884, Natalie requested a Catholic priest to perform last rites at his bedside, although he never converted in his lifetime. He was buried in the famed Père Lachaise Cemetery in Paris.

The mood in New Orleans during the war was, at first, celebratory. The first months after the surrender of Fort Sumter were a time of optimism for the city as much as they were for Charleston. The belief prevailed that the war would be short-lived. There were some Jews in New Orleans who supported secession strongly; others had doubts as to whether Louisiana should enter the Confederacy. There were also a few who took little part in the idealism of the conflict and focused on simply preserving their interests.

In late April 1862, Union forces under the command of Admiral David Farragut invaded from the Mississippi River and captured the city, handing control of the occupation over to General Benjamin F. Butler. Resistance to occupation was fierce; mobs of civilians attacked soldiers with rocks and tore the American flag from the flagpole of the United States Mint building. But Butler instilled stringent rule over the city. He required all men to swear an oath of loyalty to the United States, a requirement that led many Jews to leave the city after occupation. Among these Confederate loyalists was Reverend James Gutheim, who refused to swear the oath and moved instead to Montgomery, Alabama. Even with this movement out of the city, all four congregations existent in New Orleans during the war maintained regular services throughout the conflict.

The war significantly affected the Mississippi River and international trade routes that many Jewish businessmen in New Orleans relied on.

Trade with New York, in particular, was vital to the retail and wholesale operations that were being conducted in the area. Nearly 10 percent of Jewish businesses closed during the war due to this restriction in trade. The capture of New Orleans aided in the reopening of these lines of commerce, although illegal trade continued throughout the war. Many Jews in New Orleans and elsewhere took steps to protect their interests by stockpiling cotton in hopes that prices would increase. Some engaged in a black market that developed in the Mexican border towns of Matamoros and Boca del Rio, where cotton was traded between merchants from New Orleans, New York, Great Britain and elsewhere. Jews from other towns like Bayou Sara, Baton Rouge, Vicksburg and Natchez moved into the city seeking economic recovery and safety.

The spring of 1865 marked the end of the Civil War and the beginning of the long road of Reconstruction for New Orleans. The war affected the Jewish community in many ways. For the first time since significant waves of immigrants began arriving in the 1820s, the Jewish population of New Orleans was mostly static, which allowed time for some cohesion to develop as neighborhoods became more defined and identity more distinct. The mobility of the Jewish immigrant population waned, although the peddler tradition continued. Because the majority of Jewish businessmen in New Orleans were engaged in sales operations that relied on goods from northern cities like New York and Philadelphia, these entrepreneurs were not as affected by the economic damages of war as others were. The quality of life for New Orleans's Jewish population improved in the years following the Civil War.

CHAPTER THREE

Antebellum Mississippi and Louisiana and the Civil War

B y 1803, most of what composes present-day Louisiana and Mississippi had come under the control of the newly formed United States, with the vast Louisiana Territory reaching into the West and the Mississippi Territory comprising present-day Alabama. France and Great Britain's influence was no longer colonial but rather cultural, particularly in rural Louisiana, which was home to a large number of Acadian French exiles. The river and the land along it was still an untamed frontier that held great promise for enterprising pioneers—as long as they could survive the rigors of travel through rough trails and swamplands. Small settlements depended on trade via the river and through smaller waterways and bayous. Roads, where they existed, were treacherous and unimproved.

Much of the land to the east of the Mississippi River and south of the thirty-first parallel—including the present-day Louisiana parishes of East Baton Rouge, East Feliciana and West Feliciana—remained within Spanish West Florida. This also included the towns of Bayou Sara and Baton Rouge, which, in 1803, were small settlements along the Mississippi River, like many others that would develop in the early nineteenth century.

Although he realized most of his success years later in New Orleans, Maurice Barnett first established himself in Baton Rouge around 1806. Originally from the Netherlands, Barnett's family moved to Philadelphia when he was a child, and he was likely around thirty years old when he moved to Baton Rouge and married Marie Céleste Trahan, a Creole. His brother would later follow him to Louisiana and establish his own family in Opelousas, a town in present-day St. Landry Parish approximately sixty miles west of the Mississippi River.

Baton Rouge was a small settlement, yet it was strategically important to the various colonial powers and, eventually, the United States. By the time Maurice Barnett opened his mercantile operation, the French, British and Spanish colonial governments had consecutively controlled Baton Rouge. The settlement was home to roughly 1,500 people by 1803. The agricultural and infrastructural influences that would soon give rise to antebellum-plantation economies were falling into place, and Barnett was in a good situation to profit from them. His store carried everything from farming supplies to personal luxuries—many things that would otherwise require one to travel to the big city to buy.

Early on, Barnett built contacts with Jews who were already doing business in New Orleans. This included Alexander Hart, Asher Moses Nathan and Ruben Rochelle. He purchased goods from wholesalers in New Orleans and transported them upriver to his store in Baton Rouge. By 1810, many New Orleans–based merchants followed suit, including Nathan, who opened an additional store in Baton Rouge. Barnett bought property in Bayou Sara, another settlement in Spanish West Florida near what would later become St. Francisville. Bayou Sara was on its way to becoming an important economic center along the river, and Barnett was sure to establish interests in the expanding river town.

The land north of Spanish West Florida had been acquired by the United States as Mississippi Territory in 1798, five years before the Louisiana Purchase. Thus, by 1810, the settlers of Spanish West Florida, the majority of whom spoke little, if any, Spanish, were surrounded by United States territory. This precarious position between colonialism and the new republic caused a rebellion that started in the Spanish West Florida town of St. Francisville (near Bayou Sara) and spread to Baton Rouge, where Fort San Carlos was captured. The rebels declared themselves the Republic of West Florida and began establishing a government by drafting a constitution similar to the American Constitution. This republic lasted only a few weeks, however, before the territory became part of the United States. From 1810 onward, both Mississippi and Louisiana were United States territories, although Louisiana would not gain statehood until 1812, followed by Mississippi in 1817.

No evidence suggests that Maurice Barnett participated in the West Florida Rebellion, although it is very likely that this upset of river commerce would have motivated him to move to New Orleans in 1812. Baton Rouge would not become the state capital of Louisiana until 1846, and even after this, the city remained economically subordinate to New Orleans. Yet a few Jews would move to the capital city in the antebellum period, including Jacob Farrnbacher, who became a successful merchant, and Simon Mendelsohn, who was a grocer.

Other small towns along the Mississippi River may have had Jewish settlers in this early period as well; some historians suggest that other Jews were in Natchez as early as 1798, around the same time Benjamin Monsanto was in the area. Evidence also indicates that as many as twenty Jewish families lived in Vicksburg by 1825. Charles Levin of Charleston, South Carolina, was another early Jewish settler, who traveled to Woodville, Mississippi, in the late 1820s to be a schoolteacher. However, he left Mississippi after a brief tenure that included a duel with future Confederate President Jefferson Davis. Men like Charles Levin, Maurice Barnett and Benjamin Monsanto were uncommon in Mississippi and Louisiana before the 1840s. Although their presence was significant and had an impact on the communities in the area, they were nevertheless pioneers who ventured into frontier territory to seek their fortune. The real period of Jewish immigration into the delta region began in the 1830s and 1840s, at which time, nearly all the towns along the Mississippi River experienced a flux of Jewish families and businesses.

In 1812, the steamboat *New Orleans* was the first vessel of its kind to travel the Mississippi River. The improvement of trade routes along the river, as well as relative political stabilization within the new states of Louisiana and Mississippi, contributed to a boom in population. As New Orleans grew, so did the towns along the river. The town of Natchez, for example, had grown from a backwater fort in 1717 to the cosmopolitan capital of Mississippi Territory by 1812. After the introduction of steamships, which allowed merchants to send their merchandise up the river to Natchez, the wealth of the city grew even more rapidly, as did the lurid infamy of its riverside district, Natchez Under-the-Hill. Many Jews established businesses in this district, including Alsatian immigrant David Moses, who operated a cotton brokerage and general merchandise store. While Natchez became a viable way station and trading center for goods shipped along the Mississippi River, other towns like Bayou Sara, Port Gibson and Grand Gulf also participated in their share of the growing river traffic and trade in cotton.

But the economy was not the only thing booming in the Mississippi River delta; the immigrant population was also on the rise. New Orleans's Jewish population swelled during the 1840s, and many Jews who arrived in the port city continued the journey upriver to towns in Mississippi and Louisiana. Most of these immigrants were from Germany, France and the provinces of Alsace and Lorraine, although some had emigrated from Eastern Europe, Great Britain and the Caribbean. This population movement, along with concurrent waves of non-Jewish immigration (primarily Irish and German immigrants), helped to double the population of New Orleans in the 1830s, as well as increase the rural Louisianan population by more than twenty thousand. By 1850, more than 20 percent of the population of the state was foreign-born.

Like those who had traveled to New Orleans in the early nineteenth century, the Jews who left Europe to resettle along the Mississippi River did so for various reasons. Motivated by the new philosophies of the French Revolution and the reign of Napoleon Bonaparte, the French government emancipated its Jews in 1791 and, for the first time, recognized them as equal citizens. This emancipation, however, did not eradicate anti-Semitism in France, nor did it eliminate other forms of discrimination through official means. In the first two decades of the nineteenth century, French law barred any Jew from operating a business without permission from the officials of his town, and mandatory military conscription was present in both France and the German provinces. When the cost of ship passage to the United States began to decline in the 1830s, many foreigners jumped at the opportunity to emigrate across the Atlantic and establish new lives. Because many of the immigrants who settled in towns along the river spoke French, Alsatian and French Jews who journeyed to Louisiana could expect some comfort in the familiarity of the language.

Similar political and social forces motivated German Jews to emigrate. The same Enlightenment ideals that had inspired Jewish emancipation in France were the source of much contention in the German states. Opposition toward German emancipation turned violent in 1819 with the Hep-Hep riots in Bavaria and elsewhere, giving many German Jews motivation to leave. Later, the revolutions of 1848 and the famines of the 1840s would send waves of emigrants from France, Germany and Alsace-Lorraine. As more Europeans settled along the Mississippi River and sent letters and money to their families overseas, more Jews from the Old World followed to join them. The community ties that formed in the bayou, as well as those that had carried over from Europe, contributed to a tradition where new arrivals were fostered by and apprenticed to those who were more established.

Much about Louisiana and Mississippi in the antebellum period made it an ideal place for these newly arrived Jewish immigrants. Many non-Jewish immigrants arriving in the United States at the time, particularly those from Ireland and Germany, sought industrial or trade work. While this fit well into the industrial economies of the northern United States of the time, the economy of the South was based in agriculture. The reliance of the South on slave labor left little opportunity for many German and Irish laborers who were arriving in New Orleans during the 1840s. Although these immigrants often found work in occupations where slave labor would have been too expensive, Jewish immigrants arrived with a different set of skills.

Because Jews in France and Germany were not permitted to own land prior to their emancipation in Europe, they developed professions outside of agriculture. As in New Orleans, Jews along the Mississippi River opened dry-goods stores, clothing stores, grocery stores and other retail and wholesale businesses. In the rural South, where many people lived in villages far from functional infrastructure or on isolated plantations, a nearby store that provided goods without a day's journey to New Orleans would ultimately be successful. Planters, farmers, townspeople and slaves were all patrons of these small stores. As time went on, Jewish stores in towns like Natchez, Vicksburg and Baton Rouge would become crucial elements of the community. It can be reasonably assumed that the rural economic structures of Mississippi and Louisiana in the nineteenth century were supported by many of these merchants who not only provided goods for their respective townships but also engaged in the cotton and sugar trade. Yet for all the storekeepers and entrepreneurs who became successful in the first half of the nineteenth century, most began their lives in the South as peddlers, traveling across the countryside and within the towns along the Mississippi River.

The peddling tradition in European Jewish communities was well established by the time Jews began to immigrate to the United States. In fact, the appearance of Jewish peddlers in the American South was only one aspect of a nearly global phenomenon that took place as Jews left Europe and resettled across the United States, the British Isles, Argentina, Canada, South Africa, Australia and New Zealand, among other places. It was common to see a traveling Jewish peddler carrying his wares on his back or in a horse-drawn cart in Germany, Poland, Alsace-Lorraine or Lithuania, as well as other places in Central and Eastern Europe during the nineteenth century. By the 1830s and 1840s, the peddling tradition had become a part of the Jewish immigrant culture of the American South. Often, the first Jewish immigrants to arrive were young men who were either unmarried or had left their wives and families in Europe with the intention of sending for them later. In some instances, the new arrival already had family connections in Louisiana or Mississippi, usually a brother or uncle who had become established enough to open his own retail or dry-goods business. Some made their way south from New York, Philadelphia or other Atlantic ports.

For the newcomer, peddling was a temporary but profitable way of making a living with little upfront investment. The new arrival would obtain goods (such as linen, picture frames, curtains and mirrors) from retailers and wholesalers, family or otherwise, in New Orleans, Natchez, Baton Rouge or another town and set out along country roads, stopping at houses along the way to market his wares. It was in this manner that the Jewish peddler became an integral part of the southern economy. With so many scattered residences and hamlets far away from centers of commerce, customers who were both black and white welcomed the sight of the peddler.

A Jewish man from Alsace, Germany, France or Poland in the 1840s never expected to engage in peddling for very long. If he was working in partnership with a family member who owned a store, he could expect to either move up from peddling and become a clerk in town or, ideally, become financially stable enough to open his own store in a town like Bayou Sara, Clinton, Grand Gulf or Rodney. From this point, he could make enough money to send for his wife (if he had one) or pay passage for his siblings or parents to join him in America. Thus, after an initial period of wandering without the support of an immediate Jewish community, the former peddler could enjoy, once again, the structure of Jewish family life. After he accumulated enough savings, he could move into town and establish a business. This occurred not only in the delta but also across the South and in the Midwest.

When enough families moved into an area, the new Jewish community would establish a cemetery, then a congregation or benevolent association. In many instances, the congregation would become large enough to purchase a building for use as a *shtiebel* (a small, informal space for communal Jewish prayer) and, in time, construct their own formal synagogue. Yet many of the smallest communities, which were innumerable in Mississippi and Louisiana, never grew large enough to have a formal synagogue. Towns like Donaldsonville, Plaquemine, Baton Rouge and St. Francisville in Louisiana and Woodville, Port Gibson, Natchez and Vicksburg in Mississippi, however, did establish their own handsome synagogue buildings in time but not until after the Civil War.

While the course of community development in Mississippi and Louisiana towns was mostly similar, each place became home to extraordinary individuals who would be remembered for their kindness, community efforts or eccentricities. In antebellum Natchez, a number of families came together through business, personal and religious relationships to create a vibrant community that grew throughout the nineteenth century. John Mayer arrived in Natchez in 1841, but he had been a resident of New Orleans for years before that. Originally from Landau, Alsace, he changed his name from Mayer Levy to Jacob Mayer and then to John Mayer after immigrating to the United States. He was a runaway in his youth and spent years in Paris, where he worked as an apprentice and earned his trade as a shoemaker. He met his future wife, Jannette Reis, on the ship as they made their transatlantic journey to New Orleans. Jannette's parents, Eleanor and Moses Reis, also traveled to Louisiana with their children. The Mayers would eventually establish one of the most prominent Jewish families in Natchez.

John Mayer and Jannette Reis were married in New Orleans in 1835. Congregation Gates of Mercy had been established by this time, but despite the fact that the congregation and other Jewish institutions existed in the city, Moses Reis insisted on officiating his daughter's wedding ceremony in order to ensure its adherence to his Orthodox sensibilities. The couple moved to Natchez, where Mayer opened a shoe store in town.

A number of written accounts describe the Mayer home as one full of hospitality and energy. The couple had thirteen children, many of whom not only grew up to be fascinating individuals in their own right but also married other prominent members of Jewish communities in Natchez and elsewhere. Caroline Mayer, for example, married Julius Weis, the New Orleans cotton broker and philanthropist.

John Mayer himself was a community leader and was active in Natchez business and Jewish life. He was a member of the Chevra Kedusha ("Holy Society"), the early congregation of Natchez. Aaron Beekman, a German-born cotton broker and store owner who arrived in Natchez in 1843, served as its first secretary and president and was also a close friend of Mayer's. Peddlers around Natchez in the mid-nineteenth century could find rest, company and a hot meal at the Mayer house. One of John Mayer's descendants, Clara Lowenburg Moses, recalled in her memoirs that the Mayer home "was the center of all Jewish festivities, and at the long dining table (which had been bought from Judge Thatcher and at which George Washington had once dined) there were often seated as many as thirty-five guests on Passover Eve, the feast of Seder, which was always celebrated with much pomp and ceremony." John Mayer's family would continue to be a pivotal element in the Jewish community of Natchez throughout the Civil War and into the Reconstruction era.

Antebellum Mississippi and Louisiana and the Civil War

One of the oldest trade and travel routes in the country, the Natchez Trace played a crucial role in the settling of the colonial and antebellum South. The United States Army began work on the road in 1801, when much of the territory it ran through was still being disputed between the colonial powers and Native American tribes. Known in its day as the "Devil's Backbone" because of its location on a winding ridge, the Natchez Trace connected Natchez with Nashville, Tennessee, and allowed settlers to travel into and from the Mississippi Territory. It also fostered the wild nature of the Mississippi frontier by giving land pirates, highwaymen and thieves an unenforced route to travel between territories, which cultivated Natchez Under-the-Hill's bad reputation. But much like Louisiana Highway 1 would do in the nineteenth century, the Trace's route helped determine the location and prosperity of towns along the river.

The town of Port Gibson, for example, was close to the Mississippi River but was also located along the Trace and was a popular stop along the way for peddlers and those who brought goods southward to Natchez. Like many towns in Mississippi, Port Gibson was a wayside and a commercial hub in an area that was too far from commercial centers like Vicksburg and Natchez for settlers, farmers, planters and their families to acquire goods on a regular basis. Although it never developed to become a large town, it was a significant rural center in the antebellum period that boasted a number of saloons, inns and stores that travelers and townspeople alike could access. The town was successful enough in the first half of the nineteenth century that, when the capital of Mississippi was moved from Natchez in the early 1820s, Port Gibson was considered for the new location (the city of Jackson, however, would eventually be founded in order to fill this need). Port Gibson was roughly ten miles away from the Mississippi River and, thus, became more of a banking and mercantile center than a port city. By 1846, the town was home to 965 people.

Jews who arrived in Port Gibson in the 1830s and 1840s owned many of the town's stores and other businesses. It was at this formative period that personal and business ties were developed, creating a complicated fabric of relationships across these small towns. The Ullmans and Geisenbergers are one example. Both the Ullmans and the Geisenbergers were from the same area of Alsace-Lorraine and maintained close ties in the United States, settling in Port Gibson in the 1840s. Like many emigrants from the German states, Jacob Ullman and his family moved to the United States in order to escape tyranny in their home province. Jacob's brother, Isaac, had already settled in Port Gibson, and the two brothers operated a butcher shop until 1853, when Isaac and his wife died of yellow fever. Jacob Ullman and his wife raised their nieces and nephews along with their own children. Wolf and Fanny Geisenberger began their life in Port Gibson but moved to Natchez in the 1850s after Wolf accumulated enough money from his business. Some of the Ullman children would also move to Natchez and become part of an intricate network of Jewish communities around the Mississippi River, which were made stronger by intermarriage and the arrival of new immigrants from Europe.

Like the Ullmans and the Geisenbergers, Samuel Bernheimer's children in Port Gibson would eventually seek their fortune in other towns, such as St. Louis, Missouri, and Mobile, Alabama, where they would meet and marry other Jews and start their own families. Samuel Bernheimer himself was born in Austria in 1812 and immigrated to New York in the mid-1840s. From New York, he traveled to Charleston, South Carolina, and then to New Orleans. He was a peddler and settled in Woodville, Mississippi, for a time before opening a store in Liberty, Mississippi. He married in Liberty, and he and his wife moved to Port Gibson in 1847. Over the next few years, his two brothers, Jacob and Adolph, would come from Austria to join him in his dry-goods business, Bernheimer & Bros.

Grand Gulf, roughly a dozen miles west of Port Gibson, was the site of the first Jewish cemetery in the area, which was utilized by Jews in both Grand Gulf and Port Gibson until the town was effectively abandoned after the Civil War. The town's Jewish population (roughly seventeen) helped establish congregation Gemiluth Chassed in Port Gibson in 1859, which met at the Odd Fellows Hall in town until Reconstruction, when the congregation built its own synagogue. Grand Gulf was only one of many towns that had a Jewish presence in the antebellum period, but the Jewish community there did not grow large enough to foster its own congregation.

Grand Gulf was also one of many towns along the river that were destroyed and abandoned over the course of the nineteenth century. Ever unfortunate, Grand Gulf seemed to suffer every calamity imaginable. In its time, the small town handled more cotton commerce along the river than Vicksburg and Natchez combined and was a hub of culture and business. Along its seventy-six town blocks, the town sported "three hotels, five taverns, a distillery, a theatre, a slave auction block, two tinsmiths, a gunsmith, a jeweler, six doctors, two surgeons, an obstetrician, two dentists, and handled thirty-five steamboats a week." But a number of yellow fever epidemics combined with the ravages of the Civil War led to the town's eventual abandonment. About a decade before the war began, several steamboat explosions (which were common along the Mississippi River in those days) destroyed a portion of Grand Gulf's wharves, and a number of yellow fever epidemics in the 1850s depleted the population considerably. But the greatest blow to the once-lively town came when the Mississippi River changed course and consumed more than fifty of the town's blocks between 1855 and 1860. Many residents lost their homes and businesses, including the Jews who lived in Grand Gulf. Most relocated to Port Gibson and other towns following this disaster; others moved away when the town became a major theater of the Siege of Vicksburg.

While cotton was king along the entirety of the river, the cultivation of sugar cane was also a booming agricultural industry in areas around the mouth of the river. These towns were part of the same river-trade network as Natchez, Vicksburg and Port Gibson, but some also utilized additional available waterways to open up trade. Donaldsonville, Louisiana, was one of those towns. Donaldsonville is located not only along the banks of the Mississippi River but also on the edge of Bayou Lafourche, a slow-moving river that stretches from Donaldsonville southeast to the town of Thibodeaux. By the 1850s, Ascension Parish, where Donaldsonville is located, was surrounded by sugar cane plantations. Compared to cotton, sugar cane was significantly more labor intensive and required more acreage. Between the 1850s and 1860s, the average sugar cane plantation grew from 460 acres to 800 acres. Ascension Parish was no exception, and in fact, most of it was under cultivation, which led to Donaldsonville becoming a center of commercial and cultural activity.

Henry Hyams, the cousin of Judah P. Benjamin, was one of a number of prominent Jews who spent time in Donaldsonville. In the 1830s, he worked as a clerk at the Canal Bank and eventually became a wealthy landowner and politician. Other active Jewish businessmen in Donaldsonville include Henry Pforzheimer, Maas Tobias and Abraham Klotz from Germany, Poland and Alsace, respectively.

The large sugar cane plantations in Ascension Parish and the surrounding countryside created a market for Jewish peddlers who traveled through the area in the decades preceding the Civil War. This area was where Leon Godchaux first peddled household items to plantation residents in the 1830s. He opened his first store in 1840 at the age of sixteen, in the town of Convent in neighboring St. James Parish. He was by no means the only peddler to become established in this area, but he did enjoy a long and successful career.

Jacob Lehmann was another Jewish peddler who would rise to success in the retail and sugar industries of Donaldsville. Lehmann came to Donaldsonville from Germany in 1836. With a total population of about five hundred, Donaldsonville in the 1830s had a significant Jewish community. After arriving in the United States, Jacob Lehmann changed his name to Lemann and began establishing connections in New York; Cincinnati, Ohio; and Newport, Rhode Island, as well as within Ascension Parish. Like many Jews who owned retail and dry-goods stores in Louisiana and Mississippi, Lemann catered not only to the needs of planters and townspeople but also to slaves and free people of color. He also supplied peddlers with products to sell on their routes through rural Louisiana. But while many Jews who settled in river towns remained mobile, opened branch stores and maintained continued trade relationships with other townships, Jacob Lemann settled in Donaldsonville and planted deep roots. He married Marie Esther Ber de Lot, a Creole, during the 1840s and bought real estate around Donaldsonville. His identity as a southerner did not supersede his Jewish identity, however. After his arrival in Louisiana, Jacob Lemann kept his business records and ledgers in Yiddish, and this likely provided him both some confidentiality and comfort, as Yiddish was his first language. He frequently purchased goods from Jewish-owned businesses in New

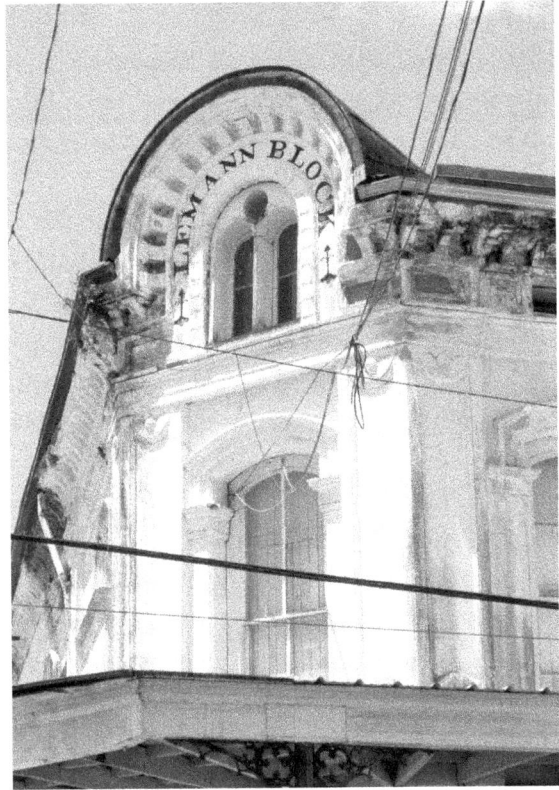

The Lemann Block, built by Jacob Lemann in Donaldsonville, Louisiana. *Photograph by Emily Ford.*

Orleans and elsewhere, including Leon Godchaux's New Orleans store. In 1852, while visiting New York with Marie, she converted to Judaism before a rabbinical court led by Dr. Max Lilienthal and changed her name to Miriam.

The antebellum-plantation economy in which Jewish store owners, brokers, factors and other businesses operated was heavily reliant on credit. In the case of both cotton and sugar cane, the planter or farmer would not receive a payout for his crop until its harvest. In the meantime, depending on the size and nature of the operation, the planter or farmer would need to purchase everything himself, from household goods and farm equipment to clothes and food for his slaves. Oftentimes, the store owner would maintain credit for his clients over the course of the growing season and expect the debt to be settled at the harvest. This system was so pervasive that as much as 70 percent of all goods purchased by farmers in Natchez during the antebellum period was obtained through credit.

Furthermore, once the cotton or sugar cane crop was harvested, the issue of transport to market would need to be handled. In addition, farmers would need to hire a factor, or purchasing agent, to sell their product for the best price.

Because credit was essential to doing business in the cash-poor South, Jewish storekeepers often accepted cotton as payment to satisfy a planter's debt and, using connections in New Orleans and elsewhere, engaged in the speculation and brokerage of cotton themselves. These trends not only created another niche in which Jews in Louisiana and Mississippi were essential to the economy, but they also made clear the delicacy of the economy as a whole. In years when cotton or sugar cane crops suffered, a planter might not be able to pay off his debt, causing a domino effect that led to greater events, such as the Panic of 1837. The emancipation of slaves during the Civil War would also cause devastation to this system as the labor that powered the southern economy dissipated, and this, in turn, upset the intricate network of credit lines that supported it. A number of Jews in the Mississippi River delta were affected by these changes in the southern economy, and in the years after the war, they would find themselves in quite a unique situation.

For the planters and traders who lived farther away from the river's banks and had to make long trips to places like Natchez or Grand Gulf for provisions and entertainment, the process of transporting goods to the river was strenuous. The introduction of railroad lines in Louisiana and Mississippi, however, did provide easier access to the river and the towns along its banks. Additionally, the rail lines facilitated travel between towns, and this helped new and existing Jewish communities grow along the delta. Moreover, the connectivity provided by the railroad created a larger Jewish network that not only led to new business partnerships but also allowed for courtship and marriage between individuals from different towns.

One of the first rail lines to be established along the Mississippi River was the West Feliciana Railroad, which connected the towns of Woodville, Mississippi, and St. Francisville, Louisiana, in 1831. St. Francisville is located on bluffs above the Mississippi River north of Baton Rouge, and Bayou Sara was just below St. Francisville on the river's banks. The establishment of the West Feliciana Railroad brought Jews to the town in the 1840s, but the Jewish community of St. Francisville didn't grow significantly until after the Civil War. Woodville, much like St. Francisville and Bayou Sara, was a way station, and many peddlers who traveled along the river settled there, especially after the West Feliciana Railroad connected the town to other river communities. Other towns along the river, such as Port Gibson and Natchez, also grew as a result of the rail lines and the connectivity they provided.

In 1848, two peddlers, Jacob Cohen and Jacob Schwartz, bought a plot of land outside Woodville in order to establish a Jewish cemetery and bury their compatriot, Henry Burgance, who had died suddenly. The cemetery, later known as Beth Israel Cemetery after the town's congregation, was used until sometime in the first half of the twentieth century. As in many other towns, the establishment of a Jewish cemetery preceded the formation of a congregation. In time, Woodville would come to be known as "Little Jerusalem" because of its flourishing Jewish community.

The town of Plaquemine, located downriver from Baton Rouge, followed a similar course of events. Jewish businesses in the town thrived off of commerce from the river. With the development of the Plaquemine Hebrew Benevolent Society, services were organized in private homes until a building was found near the Mississippi Riverfront. The society also established a cemetery at the intersection of Federal and Division Streets.

Like Woodville's Beth Israel Cemetery, the Plaquemine cemetery still tells the story of its early settlers today. Numerous headstones identify birthplaces such as Alsace, Lorraine and Germany. Families like the Levys, Kowalskis and Meyers worked to not only build successful businesses in Plaquemine but also create a foundation for Jewish life and community in what was then a frontier town. The congregation held services at a purchased building near the Mississippi River into the late 1870s.

Vicksburg may have been the first town among those discussed to establish regular services for its Jewish community. There were roughly twenty-five Jewish families in Vicksburg by 1840, and although they worshipped in private homes, they were organized and led by a dedicated man who eventually made room in his building on Levee Street for the purposes of holding services. Bernard Yoste (sometimes spelled Barnard Yoste) was born in Charlesville, France, in 1805. He was living in Vicksburg by 1840 and had developed some wealth in real estate and other ventures, much of which he returned to the community through philanthropy. He also acted as spiritual leader for the Jews of Vicksburg during this time. He was not trained as a rabbi, but as previously mentioned, most southern congregations did not employ formally trained rabbis until after the Civil War. Establishing a place of worship, however informal, was a large step for Vicksburg at such an early time in Mississippi. Furthermore, the Jewish community in the city was observant and, unlike most other towns in the area, including New Orleans, at the time, had the services of a *shochet* to provide ritually slaughtered kosher meat.

In 1841, the group of Vicksburg Jews who had gathered for informal services at Levee Street organized one of the first Jewish congregations in Mississippi, if not the oldest. Vicksburg's congregation, known originally as the Hebrew Benevolent Congregation of the Men of Mercy, was eventually renamed Congregation Anshe Chesed in 1862. Like most of the towns along the Mississippi River, Vicksburg would not have a purpose-built synagogue until after the Civil War. The first cemetery for the congregation, established in the 1820s, was most likely located within Vicksburg's city limits, although its original address is unclear. After the Civil War, the Kiersky brothers purchased a tract of land directly beside the former battlefield (now Vicksburg National Military Park) for use as a cemetery. The cemetery, which sits beside Anshe Chesed's most recent synagogue, is still in use today.

By the mid-1830s, the Jews of Vicksburg had established an important cultural infrastructure in Jewish and non-Jewish communities alike. By 1832, Vicksburg had a Jewish member of city government, M.A. Levy, who served as selectman in that year and the year after. Other men who arrived in the 1830s and 1840s included Lazarus Baer, Abraham Aaron, Louis Levy, Simon Metzger and Julius Hornthal. The families of these men became significant members of Vicksburg's Jewish community.

One of the best-known Jewish individuals among this group was Philip Sartorius, who emigrated from Bavaria to Vicksburg in 1845. His brothers Isaac and Jacob had already established themselves in Mississippi, and Jacob had already brought one Torah scroll to Vicksburg for the new congregation to use. Philip brought the second when he left Bavaria with his sister Caroline. The two Torah scrolls brought to Mississippi by the Sartorius brothers are still housed at the Anshe Chesed synagogue. Philip Sartorius himself became a well-established business owner in Vicksburg and eventually served in the Civil War. He kept a diary while in service, and his writings are still well known and referenced among academics today.

The Jews of Natchez purchased a plot in Natchez City Cemetery in 1840, which was also utilized by members of the Jewish community of Port Gibson. Grand Gulf also had a small cemetery by the 1840s. The Jewish community of Donaldsonville established Bikur Sholim Cemetery on St. Patrick Street in 1856, and Baton Rouge would have a Jewish cemetery by 1858. Among the towns discussed, which would all develop a congregation and a purpose-built synagogue in time, St. Francisville was the only one not to have a Jewish cemetery in the antebellum period. It wasn't until 1891 that local Jewish businessman and community leader Julius Freyhan purchased land for use as a cemetery. The town's first congregation, Temple Sinai, was formed ten years later.

As previously mentioned, Jewish congregations and benevolent societies tended to form shortly after the community established a cemetery, beginning with Vicksburg in 1841. Congregations served religious and social functions in delta towns, providing religious services and aid to newly arrived immigrants. The Jews of Natchez formed the Chevra Kedusha in the 1840s, which would become congregation B'nai Israel after the Civil War. Jews in Woodville formed their first congregation in 1849, and that same year, the Jewish community of Donaldsonville began organizing services in private homes. (Its formal congregation, Hebrew Bikur Cholim of the Parish of Ascension, would not be established until 1860.) The Hebrew Benevolent Society of Plaquemine was formed in 1856, the same year as its cemetery. Finally, the Hebrew Congregation of the City of Baton Rouge, later known as Shaare Chesed, was established in 1859.

It is estimated that some six hundred Jews lived in Mississippi by 1860, while Louisiana is thought to have had a Jewish population of roughly eight thousand. In each town along the river, in both Louisiana and Mississippi, Jews from Alsace, Lorraine, Germany and elsewhere were arriving and trying their hand at various enterprises. Some were met with success; others moved on. Regardless, these individuals had to contend with the unpredictable nature of the plantation economy, diseases like yellow fever and the river itself in their efforts to build lives on the frontier. As these communities grew, their members not only established a Jewish identity within their respective towns but also maintained ties with each other, creating an important regional network that continued to grow over the course of the nineteenth century. When the Civil War broke out, many Louisiana and Mississippi Jews fought for their adopted and native homes, changing the balance of economic and social life in the South in the process.

In 1861, the states of Louisiana and Mississippi were home to a substantial population of Jewish Southerners, and when the first shots were fired in Charleston Harbor that year, many backed the Confederate cause. There were many reasons both Jewish and non-Jewish young men rallied to support the Confederacy, but for Southern Jews, the added freedom and equality they enjoyed in the South inspired their loyalty. Many Jewish historians have come to the conclusion that the Southern states were more welcoming of immigrant Jews in the nineteenth century than the states of New England and the North in general. Robert Rosen, author of *The Jewish Confederates*, points out that some of the best-known New England abolitionists of the time were themselves anti-Semitic. This contrast gave Jews in Mississippi and Louisiana added reason to defend their adopted homeland.

Jewish communities along the Mississippi River and in the South in general were, in the words of Bertram Korn, "indistinguishable from their non-Jewish neighbors," and a number of them owned slaves. Jews were extremely unlikely to become planters—the primary occupation of large slave owners—in the antebellum South. With the exception of Judah P. Benjamin, who owned Belle Chasse Plantation, south of New Orleans, and J. Levy of Donaldsonville, there were no other known Jewish plantation owners between New Orleans and Vicksburg. Numerous store owners and other businessmen owned slaves, however. In Port Gibson,

Leon Fischel (1835–1874) in his uniform. During the Civil War, Fischel served in the Confederate army as an aide to General Albert Sidney Johnston. *Goldring-Woldenberg Institute of Southern Jewish Life.*

Samuel Bernheimer and Louis Kiefer each owned at least one slave. The ratio of Jewish slave owners to the number of Jews in the South prior to 1865 was approximately the same as the ratio of white slave owners. Although it is impossible to know how many Jewish individuals disagreed with slavery, it is not surprising that there were not any Jewish abolitionists in either state, as states' rights, secessionism and slavery were all part of Southern culture at the time.

One family in Louisiana did avoid involvement in the Civil War entirely, although this was likely for practical reasons rather than moral objection. Jacob Lemann left Donaldsonville for New York in the 1850s. For the next dozen years or so, he lived elsewhere and eventually moved with his wife and son, Bernard, to Paris in 1861. While in Paris, he kept company with others who had become expatriates waiting out the war at a distance. In August 1862, Union Admiral Farragut, who had by this time helped to capture New Orleans, organized a bombardment of

Donaldsonville from the river. The town was devastated. In the next year, Bernard Lemann traveled to Donaldsonville to survey the condition of his family's business. Both Bernard and his father made periodic visits to manage their interests during the war, but neither ever served the Confederacy. In fact, Bernard formally swore allegiance to the Union during his visit, which would allow the Lemanns to maintain their property during Reconstruction.

Numerous congregations in Louisiana and Mississippi, which had formed only years before the outbreak of hostilities, were put on hold as Jews joined the ranks of the Confederate army or relocated to New Orleans, which was considered relatively safe in Union hands. Baton Rouge surrendered to the Union in May 1862 without violence, but tensions between citizens and Federal occupiers continued throughout the war. The small Baton Rouge congregation, at the time known simply as the Hebrew Congregation of the City of Baton Rouge, dispersed during the war, although some evidence shows that they met sporadically. Like the congregations of New Orleans, families saw their sons and fathers go to war, and many towns, such as Vicksburg and Port Gibson, served as battle sites. Many were also laid to waste, namely Donaldsonville and Grand Gulf. Jewish communities in every town, however, contributed soldiers to the Rebel armed forces.

It has been estimated that one thousand to ten thousand Jews served in the Confederate army (the figure varies greatly due to a lack of reliable data). The Confederate army did not record the religion of its soldiers. However, according to Robert Rosen, it is probable that between two thousand and three thousand Southern Jews served the Confederacy. Although Bernard Lemann did not join, two brothers from New Orleans—Eugene Henry and Julian Levy—both served in the Donaldsonville Artillery. Among the Levys' ranks was another Donaldsonville resident, Abraham Klotz. Born in Alsace, Klotz had worked in both Plaquemine and Iberville before moving to Donaldsonville, where he joined the Donaldsonville Artillery in 1861. Samuel Ullman, who had emigrated from Germany to Port Gibson with his parents in 1842 when he was just two years old, enlisted as a soldier in Company G, Sixteenth Mississippi, where he served under General Thomas Jonathan "Stonewall" Jackson. A

Woodville native, Gabe Kahn joined Company K, Sixteenth Mississippi, as a bugler. Colonel Leon Dawson Marks, who led the Twenty-seventh Louisiana Regiment, was born in Bayou Sara in 1829 and was already a veteran of the Mexican War by the time he served the Confederacy. He was one of the highest-ranking Jewish Confederates from Louisiana and died in September 1863 from complications from wounds he received three months before during the Siege of Vicksburg.

In 1854, Philip Sartorius met and married Sophie Rose and worked as a storekeeper and postmaster in Milliken's Bend, Louisiana, outside of Vicksburg. He joined the Fifteenth Louisiana Cavalry Battalion in 1863 but was wounded soon after at the Battle of Milliken's Bend (which was part of the Siege of Vicksburg) and taken prisoner. In his memoirs, he despaired at his fellow soldiers' treatment of one another and their behavior in the towns that they passed through, as well as how ill equipped

Philip Sartorius (1831–1913) with his wife, Sophie (1835–?). *Goldring-Woldenberg Institute of Southern Jewish Life.*

his regiment was. To him, the war was a waste. Sartorius returned home with a disabled hand and more mental scars than he had bargained for. Nevertheless, he continued to make a life for himself and his family in Vicksburg as a successful merchant and businessman.

Simon Mayer of Natchez, who joined the Natchez Light Infantry in 1861 and rose to the rank of lieutenant by 1862, did not share Sartorius's brutal assessments of war. A passionate and dedicated soldier, Mayer wrote his younger brother, Henry, to join the fight with him "with light heart & strong arms, backed by a determination to do or die." A man of short stature (he was hardly five feet tall), he was sometimes referred to as "the Little Mississippi Major," although no evidence suggests he attained such a rank. He was, however, remembered as a compassionate man who would dismount his horse and allow a wounded soldier to ride. The rest of Simon Mayer's family—his father, John; his mother, Jannette; and his many brothers and sisters—tended to affairs as much as they could in his absence. They wrote to their son, ran the family shoe store and continued to hold High Holy Day services at their house, although an engine house on North Union Street was sometimes used for this purpose as well. John Mayer, concerned with the risks of being so close to town and the river, especially after Vicksburg was captured, organized a number of men to guard the town and monitor activities on the river's banks. In fact, he was so worried about the war coming too close to home that he purchased a house in the town of Washington (outside Natchez) and relocated his family there. He stayed in the town and took care of his store with the help of his older children Henry, Emma and Ophelia.

On September 2, 1862, after stopping in Natchez for supplies, the Union gunboat *Essex* was fired upon by John Mayer's home guard, which mistakenly took the boat's docking as offensive action. Occurrences like this in towns near the Mississippi River were somewhat common. In both Donaldsonville and Baton Rouge, Union navy vessels returned fire. In the case of Natchez, the *Essex* shelled the town from the river, damaging structures and causing the mayor to surrender the town to Federal control. The only casualty of the hour-long shelling of Natchez was Rosalie, the seven-year-old daughter of Aaron Beekman. In her memoirs, Clara Lowenburg Moses described seeing the Beekmans running from their home in Natchez Under-the-Hill. Rosalie was struck by a shard from an exploding shell and was taken by her cousin, Miriam Wexler, to the Mayers' home on Main Street. Despite the families' efforts to treat her wounds, she died that night. She was buried in the Jewish section of Natchez City Cemetery.

Once Natchez was surrendered to Federal forces, Union soldiers took residence in the town. Sutlers, men who sold provisions to these soldiers, were often seen accompanying Union troops as they traveled through the South. Among these men were Henry Frank and Isaac Lowenburg, both of whom were Jewish Northerners who arrived in Natchez in 1863 with their compatriot, John Hill. They became friends with John Mayer and joined the family for High Holy Days services, and both men stayed in Natchez after the war. By 1865, Samuel Ullman of Port Gibson arrived in Natchez as well and joined the Natchez Jewish community by marrying John Mayer's daughter Emma. In time, the other two men would marry into the family: Isaac Lowenburg married Ophelia Mayer, and Henry Frank married Melanie Mayer.

The Mayer women not only maintained lively households during Federal occupation but were also strong Confederate supporters. Ophelia, who was ardent in her convictions to the Southern cause, was reprimanded by occupying Union officials for writing a letter that described occupying Union General Mason Brayman as a "miserable tyrant." Along with a number of other women, she was briefly imprisoned at Natchez City Hall, until Isaac Lowenburg and Henry Frank arranged to have her freed. General Brayman was, in fact, a strict and unreasonable occupier. When a Natchez Catholic bishop refused to pray for President Abraham Lincoln, the general exiled him to Vidalia, Louisiana, just across the river from the city.

Regardless of the consequences of defending Confederate soldiers, Jannette Mayer and her daughters continued to make every effort to help Simon and his compatriots. The following entry from the memoir of Clara Lowenburg Moses describes one instance in which Jannette, Emma and Caroline smuggled supplies to their friends in gray:

Once during the war the soldier boys had written home that they needed boots, shoes, socks, shirts, trousers, everything, it seemed, but how could such contraband goods be sent to Confederate soldiers? A fine scheme was planned. Our friend, Henry Frank, promised to get passes for mother, Emma, and Carrie to pass through the Union guards at the city limits, where friends living in the country would meet them and forward the clothes. Fortunately, the women in those days wore great hoop skirts, and under these, around their waists, mother, Emma, and Carrie hung all the needed articles. Thus laden, they were helped into the carriage, and were driven to the city limits, where the passes had to be examined. With fear and trembling, Emma handed the guard the papers. Imagine her delight when she noticed that he was trying to read them upside down! "Any contraband goods?" and all being fair in love and war, they answered "No." "Drive on then and have a nice day with your friends," was the pleasant rejoinder of the ignorant unsuspecting guard.

By the time Robert E. Lee surrendered to Ulysses S. Grant at Appomattox in April 1865, the entire cultural and economic structure of the South was crumbling. Reconstruction would soon begin, and with it would come great change for the people of delta towns like Natchez, Port Gibson, Woodville, Plaquemine and St. Francisville. Population movements were widespread and far-reaching. Opportunistic carpetbaggers who were moving in from the North and the diaspora of newly freed African Americans changed the southern landscape dramatically. But over the course of the next thirty-five years and into the twentieth century, the Jewish communities on the Mississippi River would grow and enjoy great successes in philanthropy and commerce. Many would form new congregations, reorganize those that had already been established and build synagogues and schools. Some of these communities, however, would also suffer the rise of southern nativism and anti-Semitism. That so many of their sons sacrificed their lives—and so many more had risked theirs—for the defense of the lost cause remained a point of pride in these small-town Jewish communities, one that members of each southern Jewish community hoped would not be forgotten.

CHAPTER FOUR

Jewish New Orleans in the New South and the Twentieth Century

The decline in Jewish immigration during the Civil War created greater cohesion among Jews who were already living in the city. It was during this time that Jewish identity evolved and became distinctly New Orleanean. As new generations of Jews grew up in the city, they invested in the prosperity of not only their coreligionists but also the New Orleans community as a whole: they had become an important, contributing ingredient of the local gumbo melting pot. The number of associations and charities increased, as did the number of synagogues within the city. Overall, the Jewish community matured and continued to do so throughout the twentieth century.

In 1867, the Gates of Prayer synagogue on Jackson Avenue in the suburb of Lafayette was finally completed. Two of the city's other three synagogues—Tememe Derech and Dispersed of Judah—were located in neighborhoods very near to the new Gates of Prayer, which was once considered a suburban congregation. Suburban Lafayette had been incorporated into the city of New Orleans as the Garden District neighborhood. As time passed, Jews would continue to move farther uptown. Tememe Derech remained on the 500 block of Carondelet Street in the American Sector, and Dispersed of Judah continued to hold services at its own synagogue, which was also on Carondelet. Only Gates of Mercy remained on the other side of Canal Street in what is today

Gates of Prayer synagogue, built in 1867. *From* Israelites of Louisiana: Their Religious, Civic, Charitable and Patriotic Life, *1904. Louisiana Research Collection, Tulane University.*

the Tremé neighborhood, and it was somewhat removed from what were quickly becoming the city's most popular neighborhoods for congregants.

The Dryades neighborhood, which had begun to evolve into an identifiable Jewish area in the 1850s, continued to develop after the Civil War. By the 1880s, this part of what is now the Central City and Garden District neighborhoods of New Orleans was home to Jews from Poland, Russia, Lithuania, Romania and other areas of Eastern Europe who had escaped the intensely anti-Semitic political climate of their homeland. The cultural contrasts between the newly arrived Orthodox Jews from Eastern Europe and the predominantly German, Alsatian and Sephardic families who had become established in New Orleans created distance between the two communities, with the Orthodox Jews rooted in the Dryades "Muses" area of the city and the German communities remaining near St. Charles Avenue and operating businesses in the French Quarter and around Canal Street.

The Dryades district became New Orleans's only distinct Jewish neighborhood. The area never grew to become a large neighborhood, and only a small percentage of the Jewish population in the Crescent City lived there. The street was nevertheless a center for Jewish-owned and -oriented businesses, including groceries, butchers and delicatessens, all of which provided customers with kosher fare. In fact, Jews in New Orleans had become such a significant market by the 1870s that non-Jewish-owned grocery stores throughout the city were stocking traditional Jewish foods and kosher products. That market would grow exponentially as more immigrants moved into the city and the community expanded.

The definition of American Judaism during this time was changing. Rather than composing one unified group, Jews were increasingly identifying themselves as either Orthodox or Reform. Three new Orthodox congregations were established in New Orleans. The first, Chevra Thilim, was mostly made up of Galitzianer Jews from what are now Poland and Ukraine. Although the congregation was formed in 1887, it experienced little growth and did not construct a synagogue until 1915. Many of the congregations of Eastern European immigrants in New Orleans remained small. Another small congregation, Chevra Mikveh Israel, which was primarily composed of Lithuanian immigrants, also formed in the 1880s and met for services on Carondelet Street near Poydras Street by 1900.

The third congregation to form was Agudath Achim Anshe Sfard. Founded in 1896 by Jews from Lithuania and Russia, it was originally Chasidic in tradition but became conventional Orthodox in the early twentieth century while retaining some traditions, such as the Nusach Sfard liturgy. Like many of the smaller congregations of Eastern European Jews, members of Anshe Sfard attended services in rented buildings and private homes until 1900, when a building on South Rampart Street near Erato Street was purchased for use as a synagogue. In 1925, the congregation moved once more, this time to a purpose-built synagogue designed by Jewish architect Emile Weil, who would design a number of other synagogues in New Orleans. Although the Dryades neighborhood shifted away from being a Jewish area by the middle of

Agudath Achim Anshe Sfard, interior, designed in 1925 by architect Emile Weil. *Congregation Agudath Achim Anshe Sfard.*

the twentieth century, the grand synagogue building at 2230 Carondelet Street continues to be the home of Anshe Sfard.

The dynamism among the multiple nationalities that made up Orthodox congregations in late nineteenth-century New Orleans prompted the formation of another synagogue in 1904. Tememe Derech, an Eastern European congregation near the Dryades neighborhood, had remained small since its formation in 1857. In 1904, the congregation merged with a number of other Orthodox congregations to form Beth Israel. The next year, the new congregation purchased a mansion on Carondelet Street, which was farther uptown than the facility once used by Tememe Derech. In 1924, the mansion at 1616 Carondelet was demolished, and a new building, also designed by Emile Weil, was constructed. Similar in style to the Anshe Sfard synagogue, the building's wide brick façade is embellished with white plastered surrounds and geometric accents. Like other Jewish houses

Beth Israel, built in 1924. *Photograph by Emily Ford.*

of worship designed by Weil, the apex of the building is adorned with two tablets inscribed in Hebrew. Although Beth Israel, like many other congregations, relocated to the suburbs (Lakeview, a neighborhood at the edge of New Orleans, by Metairie) in the latter half of the twentieth century, its former synagogue near Carondelet and Terpsichore Streets remains.

The years between the 1870s and 1920s were a time of definition for American Judaism as a whole. With Jewish communities growing and experiencing various degrees of assimilation, religious leaders grappled with questions regarding tradition and adaptation. American culture was dramatically different from the segregated, tightknit Jewish society that had developed in European ghettos. Rabbis who were participating in the discussion argued whether traditional rabbinical law was relevant in America. In particular, they discussed the importance of *kashrut* (the laws of kosher eating), and some argued that such compliance would be impossible in isolated communities in the United States. Many second-generation

American Jews saw the rituals of their fathers to be overly strict and time consuming. This, among other trends, led to a number of identity-shaping events among Jewish communities in the United States and New Orleans.

In the North, Jewish leaders like Rabbi Isaac Mayer Wise were working toward a unification of congregations in the United States. Isaac Leeser's efforts to improve cooperation among American congregations ended with his death in 1868. Wise became posthumously known as the undisputed leader of the Reform movement, thanks in large part to his *Minhag America* prayer book. He also led the movement to form the Union of American Hebrew Congregations in 1873. In New Orleans, debates regarding Reform centered on a number of leaders from each respective congregation, but the greatest contrast existed between Rabbi Bernard Illowy and Reverend James Gutheim.

After arriving in the country in 1850 from Germany and leading congregations in numerous synagogues (most of which were in the Northeast), Bernard Illowy came to New Orleans in 1861 to lead Gates of Mercy. Although considered a strict, uncompromising conservative who balked at the notion of Reform, Rabbi Illowy recognized that many Jewish traditions and practices had become obsolete and were hardly observed among American Jews, particularly in New Orleans where many had assimilated into the greater culture. While he contributed to the dialogue of the Reform movement, Bernard Illowy was primarily remembered in New Orleans for his inability to compromise and his austere attitude toward his congregants. He remained at Gates of Mercy for only four years and, in 1865, left New Orleans completely. In his 1922 retrospect of the Reform movement in New Orleans, Rabbi Max Heller observed, "That the man of genuine scholarship was out of place in the pioneer environment was shown by the career of…Bernard Illowy."

James Gutheim, in contrast to Illowy, was determined to help shape the American Jewish identity. According to documents, Gutheim was present in New Orleans in the 1850s and served as spiritual leader for Gates of Mercy and, later, Dispersed of Judah. He also served a congregation in Montgomery, Alabama, after he refused to swear an oath of allegiance to the Union in New Orleans and fled the city. He returned to the Crescent City to replace Bernard Illowy at Gates of Mercy but soon left in 1868 and moved to New York. His replacement of Illowy can be interpreted as the official beginning of the Reform movement in New Orleans, but Illowy's own frustrations with the lax approach to Jewish law among his congregants indicates that such notions were already stirring.

Gutheim's brief presence in the city, however, may have prompted some Jews in New Orleans to finally establish a Reform congregation. Although already serving New York's Temple Emanuel as a reader, Gutheim corresponded with members of Gates of Mercy who felt that the pace toward Reform at their synagogue was not quick enough. In 1870, thirty-seven men met to form the new congregation that would

James K. Gutheim (1817–1886). *From* Jubilee Souvenir of Temple Sinai *by Max Heller, 1922. Temple Sinai and Louisiana Research Collection, Tulane University.*

become New Orleans's first Reform synagogue, Temple Sinai. Among the people present at the meeting were some of the most wealthy and influential Jewish men in New Orleans at the time, including Julius Weis, Leon Godchaux, Isidore Newman and Michael Frank. Frank was elected the congregation's first president, and by 1871, the construction firm of Little & Middlemiss was at work building the new Temple Sinai on Carondelet Street near Tivoli Circle, which is today known as Lee Circle. It's also worth noting that the location of the new temple was closer to the homes of some of the congregation's more affluent members.

The temple was finished in 1872. It was impressively large and ornate, which expressed the wealth and status of the congregation's members. It

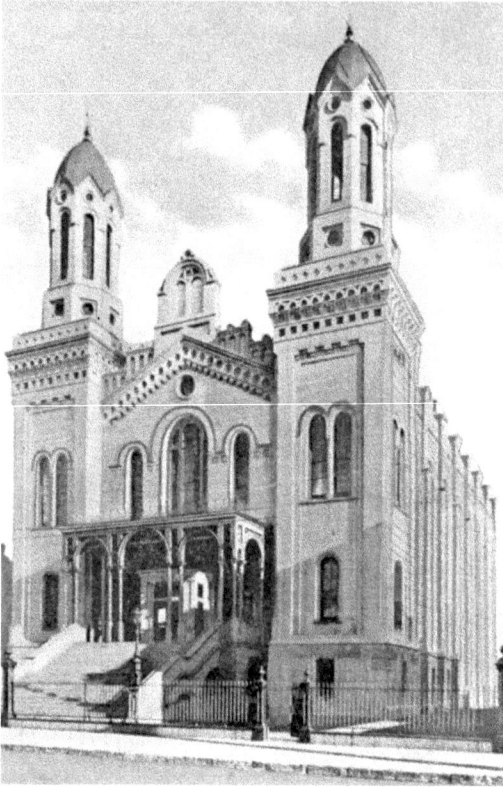

Temple Sinai, built in 1872 by Little & Middlemiss. *William A. Rosenthall Judaica Collection, Special Collections, College of Charleston.*

also featured twin Byzantine towers on each side of its primary façade that could be seen from far away. The temple itself, however, was demolished in the mid-twentieth century, but the towers were salvaged and mounted onto a residential building on Canal Street near Bottinelli Square.

Gutheim was called back to become rabbi of Temple Sinai in 1872 and officiated the consecration of the new temple. Under his leadership—along with that of Rabbi Isaac Leucht, who had served Gates of Mercy in Gutheim's absence—the congregation at Temple Sinai became a center for Jewish charity and reform. Gutheim died in 1886 and was buried in the Temple Sinai section of Metairie Cemetery, located near New Orleans's city limits. The plot, now designated as section 84 of the historic cemetery, was established in 1884, not long before his death. Gutheim was the first to be buried in this lot, which is now dotted with the monuments and names of famous men like Emile Weil, Leon Godchaux,

Isidore Newman and many others. Reverend Gutheim's epitaph—a quotation from Presbyterian minister Benjamin Morgan Palmer, who was a close friend of Gutheim's—inscribed on Gutheim's monument reads, "A man always to be found when wanted, and always to be trusted when found." Below the inscription is an abbreviated verse carved in Hebrew that is found in the first book of Samuel, 25:29: "May his soul be bound up in the bond of eternal life."

Rabbi Max Heller took up the leadership of Temple Sinai after Gutheim's death. Heller was born in Prague in 1860 and graduated from Hebrew Union College in the mid-1880s. In 1887 his mentor, Isaac Meyer Wise, asked him to go to New Orleans and lead the Reform congregation. A progressive who strongly supported charitable causes, particularly those benefitting immigrants, Heller was aware of the need for positive relationships between the Jewish community and the rest of New Orleans. He organized a Thanksgiving Day service that was jointly attended by the congregants of Temple Sinai and the Unitarian church. Sometime later, Gates of Prayer joined the two congregations, and the service became an annual tradition that continued until the First World War. At Temple Sinai's Fiftieth Jubilee (celebrated in 1922), Heller proposed that a new house of worship be built to accommodate the growing number of congregants. The congregation purchased land in the Uptown district, and a new building was erected in 1928 on St. Charles Avenue and Calhoun Street. The building is still in use today.

Heller also engaged in a monthly lecture circuit that took him to small towns in rural Louisiana, Mississippi, Texas and Alabama. Over the course of these trips, he spoke to small groups, most of which did not have synagogues of their own. He also officiated weddings, funerals and other Jewish ceremonies for various isolated communities. His diverse efforts toward building collaborative relationships between communities not only served as a tenet of good public stewardship but also helped to combat anti-Semitic attitudes in the South. Heller's career with Temple Sinai spanned forty years. Today, he is remembered as both a leader of southern Jews and an executor of Reform principles.

In the 1890s and into the twentieth century, the economically depressed rural areas of the South—especially Louisiana and Mississippi—were

Temple Sinai's current building in Uptown. *Photograph by Emily Ford.*

the stage of racist discrimination and nativist violence. While anti-Semitism did not manifest itself violently in New Orleans, the news of events in Lake Providence and Delhi, Louisiana, between 1889 and 1890; southern vigilantism in south Mississippi that left several Jewish persons dead; and the 1915 lynching of Leo M. Frank in Marietta, Georgia, caused alarm among many of New Orleans's Jews. The events in rural Louisiana and Mississippi, known as "whitecapping," were the violent acts of incensed farmers who were displeased with Jewish businessmen who hired black laborers or fellow Jews instead of whites. Although no episodes of violence occurred in New Orleans, discrimination against Jews slowly became widespread.

Following the Civil War, minority groups across the South became the targets of hate. The 1896 *Plessy v. Ferguson* U.S. Supreme Court ruling, which legitimized segregation, originated in New Orleans, a city that was infamous for its rigid adherence to Jim Crow laws. Nearly twenty years later, nativists within the state influenced the legislature to outlaw French as a primary language of instruction in schools. Louisiana, once a state that prided itself on diversity, abandoned its multiethnic identity in favor of a select group.

It was during this time that the most exclusive luncheon clubs in New Orleans—the Boston Club and the Pickwick Club—stopped accepting Jewish members. The pageantry of Mardi Gras also gradually closed to New Orleans Jews. The first king of Carnival, a tradition that was started in 1872, was a Jewish man named Lewis Salomon, and even into the 1890s, Jewish New Orleaneans like Alice Kruttschnitt served as royalty in Mardi Gras social clubs. Yet by the turn of the century, the most elite Mardi Gras organizations (known as krewes), including the Krewes of Comus and Momus, would not admit Jewish members. The Krewe of Rex, whose king is the traditional King of Carnival (as Lewis Salomon was), maintained a small number of Jewish members but never again as krewe royalty. In response to the marginalization of Jews from high-class

The Krewe of Rex passing up Camp Street, New Orleans, 1906. Rex was one of the few krewes to permit some Jews as members during the early twentieth century. *Detroit Publishing Company Collection, Library of Congress Prints and Photographs Division.*

The Harmony Club Building. *From* Israelites of Louisiana: Their Religious, Civic, Charitable and Patriotic Life, *1904. Louisiana Research Collection, Tulane University.*

social groups, the wealthy Jewish community of New Orleans instead joined the Harmony Club, an elite Jewish club with an imposing marble building at St. Charles and Jackson Avenues. These discriminations made for tensions among New Orleans's Jewish elite, particularly around Mardi Gras, but the Jewish community as a whole persevered by increasing its charitable efforts and collaboration among synagogues and other New Orleans religious groups.

After Temple Sinai was formed, congregation Gates of Mercy saw a decline in its membership. Still located on Rampart Street, which was somewhat removed from the homes and businesses of the members it retained, Gates of Mercy was at a crossroads at which it would suffer if it did not adapt to the changing climate of New Orleans's Jewish community. At the same time, Dispersed of Judah, second in age only to Gates of Mercy, was also experiencing a decline in membership due to intermarriage, the draw of the new Reform congregation and the recent ravages of yellow fever. In 1881, an agreement between the two oldest congregations in New Orleans led to their joining together to form a new Ashkenazic congregation known as Congregation Gates of Mercy of the Dispersed of Judah, which soon came to be known simply as Touro Synagogue. The new congregation met at Dispersed of Judah's building on Carondelet Street. In 1891, Touro Synagogue became the second congregation to become Reform in New Orleans.

In 1909, following its German members as they moved farther uptown, Touro Synagogue commissioned architect Emile Weil to design a new building on St. Charles Avenue. The structure, which is today a local landmark, has been the home of the Touro Synagogue congregation for over a century. Its interior houses an ark constructed of imported cedars of Lebanon, which were donated to Dispersed of Judah by Judah Touro in 1847.

The post-bellum expansion of the Jewish community in New Orleans was oriented around philanthropy and charitable associations. In 1872,

Touro Synagogue, designed in 1909 by architect Emile Weil. *William A. Rosenthall Judaica Collection, Special Collections, College of Charleston.*

Dining room of the Jewish Orphans' Home, New Orleans, early twentieth century. *Goldring-Woldenberg Institute of Southern Jewish Life.*

the Independent Order of B'nai B'rith, a charitable association that acted as a venue for Jewish identity and solidarity, opened its first branch in New Orleans. The Seventh District, as it was known, had a membership of over four thousand by 1881. B'nai B'rith became involved with Touro Infirmary and the Jewish Widows and Orphans' Home and contributed to the effort to construct a new facility at the corner of St. Charles and Peter Avenues (later renamed Jefferson Avenue). Touro Infirmary also moved to expanded facilities on Prytania Street in 1882. By 1900, an improved brick structure was built at the same site, and in the 1890s, the Touro Home for the Aged and Infirmed and Touro Infirmary's Nursing School were built.

In addition to expanding the number of hospital and orphanage services, the New Orleans Jewish community also formed social organizations. The Young Men's Hebrew Association (YMHA) was formed in the 1890s. The *Jewish Ledger*, an influential newsletter that remained in print until the early 1960s, was based in New Orleans. A number of Jewish schools developed, including one established by the Hebrew Education Society in 1866. The Communal Hebrew Society also established a school on Josephine Street in 1915, and the Menorah Talmud Torah was established by Beth Israel in 1926. The Menorah Talmud Torah building on Euterpe Street is no longer in use as a Jewish school, but the building, with its handsome Ionic columns and twin drinking fountains, still stands.

These community accomplishments were supported by substantial contributions from wealthy New Orleans merchants and businessmen. Men like Isidore Newman, Julius Weis and many of their contemporaries served as presidents of charitable boards and donors to new facilities. Touro Infirmary's Home for the Aged and Infirmed was renamed the Julius Weis Home in 1899, and Isidore Newman School, which was originally a trade and technical school for children at the Jewish Widows

Isidore Newman School, founded in 1903. *Ida Weis Friend Collection, Louisiana Research Collection, Tulane University.*

Jewish Children's Home. *Ida Weis Friend Collection, Louisiana Research Collection, Tulane University.*

Touro Infirmary during the early twentieth century. *Touro Infirmary Archive.*

and Orphans' Home (eventually called the Jewish Children's Home), became a highly regarded college preparatory school and is still held in high esteem today. The New Orleans Museum of Art opened in 1911 and was originally named for its primary benefactor, Isaac Delgado. (The museum was renamed the New Orleans Museum of Art in 1971.) The Isaac Delgado Museum of Art was the centerpiece of City Park, one of the largest urban green spaces in the United States even today. The park, which was established in 1891, was one of the many contributions of Felix Dreyfous, son of notary Abel Dreyfous. Dreyfous not only helped establish the park but also, as a state legislator, helped create an administration for flood control in the state and served as the president of the Orleans Levee Board in 1890. A street in City Park is named after him.

New Orleanean Jewish businessmen prospered in the first decade of the twentieth century, and their successes left a lasting imprint on the city's landscape. Today, Judah Touro's name is printed on flags, banners and billboards for Touro Hospital, but this is mostly the result of the contributions of men like Michael Frank and Julius Weis. Yet four men in particular stand out as commercial and philanthropic juggernauts of the late nineteenth and early twentieth centuries. One was an enterprising French peddler who became the head of a successful sugar company and department store; two were partners in what would become an iconic drugstore in New Orleans and the state of Louisiana; and finally, one was a Bessarabian immigrant who, by his sharp wit and tough tactics, shouldered his way to success as president of the United Fruit Company.

The first of these titans of enterprise, Leon Godchaux was already active in Louisiana before the Civil War. Godchaux was born in the Alsace-Lorraine region of France in 1824 and immigrated to the United States sometime around 1840, when he earned a living as a peddler. By 1844, he was able to purchase his own dry-goods store. Five years later, he moved to New Orleans and opened a clothing store that would become a New Orleans landmark by the turn of the century. Leon Godchaux was also the owner of the famous Godchaux Sugar Company, which operated in the Louisiana towns of Napoleonville, Reserve and Raceland. His innovative use of railroad technology, as well as consolidation of

Leon Godchaux (1824–1899).
From Israelites of Louisiana: Their
Religious, Civic, Charitable and
Patriotic Life, *1904. Louisiana
Research Collection, Tulane University.*

refineries, made Godchaux Sugar a Louisiana staple until it was sold to National Sugar and Refining Company in 1958.

Leon Godchaux's first retail store in New Orleans was located in the French Quarter near present-day Decatur Street. Later, he was successful enough to build his own department store on Canal Street, where many other Jewish-owned department stores, jewelers and retailers had become established. The grand building that housed Godchaux's Department Store for more than fifty years was built long after Leon Godchaux died in 1899. The 1924 building, which remains part of the Canal Street landscape, was where Godchaux's son, grandson and great-grandson operated the business until 1986, when the department store and clothing company went bankrupt. By the time the company folded, it had nearly a dozen branches throughout southeastern Louisiana.

Another Jewish-owned business had an even bigger impact on New Orleans's culture than Godchaux's Department Store. In 1905, pharmacist Gustave Katz closed the drugstore he had operated on St. Charles Avenue and Jackson Street since 1896 to start up another pharmacy on Canal Street. His new business partner was Sydney Besthoff Sr., who had come to New Orleans from Memphis to marry his new wife. Together, they opened Katz & Besthoff Drug Store (commonly known as K&B) at 732 Canal Street, amidst the department and specialty stores already established there. This first store was very quickly followed by a second Canal Street store in 1911; a third store at St. Charles and Louisiana Avenues in 1920; and a fourth in Uptown at Carrollton Avenue and Oak Street in 1923. By 1997, when the company was sold to Florida-based drugstore chain Rite Aid, there were nearly two hundred K&B stores across the South, from Texas to Florida, with fifty in the city of New Orleans alone.

In the 1920s and 1930s, Katz & Besthoff Drug Stores were well-supplied pharmacies that stocked everything from perfume and cosmetics to candy and film. In fact, K&B introduced photo processing in its stores as early as 1938. Soda fountains that also served lunch at some locations remained a K&B trademark until the late 1970s. And the pharmacist-owned store also, of course, provided over-the-counter and prescription medicines (which were checked twice for accuracy before being sold to the customer).

Better remembered than the nectar sodas and bicycle-delivery service of the early days of K&B is the store's signature sign color. Known in New Orleans as "K&B purple," Katz & Besthoff adopted the bright pinkish-lavender early in the store's history. Turn-of-the-century drugstores customarily wrapped purchased goods with paper for their customers. As family legend goes, Sydney Besthoff's wife purchased a discounted lot of purple paper to wrap up items at the new store. The color caught on with customers, and soon, everything in the store was K&B purple, including its ubiquitous circular logo. By the time the chain drugstore was sold in 1997, only the Besthoff family still had controlling interest in K&B. Sydney Besthoff Sr. had left his shares of the company to his son, Sydney Besthoff Jr., who had also become a pharmacist. When Gustave Katz died in 1940, the remaining portion of the company owned by the Katz family was sold to the Besthoffs, although the Katz name remained part of the company's title. Sydney Besthoff III, grandson of the original founder and local philanthropist, directed the sale of the K&B company. The building at K&B Plaza near Lee Circle still stands and retains the title despite the closure of K&B stores. The story of K&B is probably one of the strongest reminders of how loyal New Orleaneans are to local businesses, as historian

John Epstein observed: "Time is marked in New Orleans by anniversaries of births, deaths, hurricanes and the closing of K&B drug stores."

If the legacy of Gustave Katz and Sydney Besthoff is one of sentimentality and nostalgia, the legacy of Samuel Zemurray, the "Banana Man," is one of shrewd entrepreneurialism and has no small amount of controversy. Born in Bessarabia (now part of Moldova and Ukraine) in 1877, he changed his name from Zmurri to Zemurray in order to better assimilate. He spent his first years in the United States in Mobile, Alabama, where he bought ripe bananas off United Fruit Company ships from Honduras and sent them by rail to be sold in rural towns. Soon after, he and a partner purchased a single cargo tanker that they used to operate their own shipping company. In the 1890s, Central American fruit had become a big business and was led by Boston-based United Fruit Company. Numerous other businessmen along the Gulf Coast also engaged in the enterprise, including the Sicilian Vaccaro

Samuel Zemurray, also known as the "Banana Man" (1877–1961). *Touro Infirmary Archive.*

family in New Orleans and Zemurray's eventual father-in-law, Jacob Weinberger of Galveston, Texas, who funded what became Zemurray's Cuyamel Fruit Company in 1910. Zemurray moved to New Orleans in 1905 and operated with his partner out of an office on Camp Street.

The political power of fruit companies in Honduras and other Central American countries at the turn of the century and into the 1930s was the result of stakeholders' attempts to influence taxes and labor organization, and on occasion, they installed their own governments, which favored their profits. Zemurray's Cuyamel Fruit, Weinberger's Bluefield Banana Company and the United Fruit Company all participated in the political coups and economic manipulation in what came to be known as "banana republics." Zemurray in particular, as president of Cuyamel Fruit Company, supported the overthrow of the Honduran government and the ascension of Manuel Bonilla to the presidency, which would lead to tax breaks and other favors for Cuyamel. Ever a clever industrialist,

The Zemurray mansion. Today, the mansion is the residence of the president of Tulane University. *Photograph by Emily Ford.*

Zemurray had his sights on United Fruit Company. Cuyamel continued to grow as a company, and in the 1920s, Zemurray and his friends bought small amounts of United Fruit stock, slowly gaining a significant stake in the company with their shares combined. He sold Cuyamel to United Fruit in 1930 and retired to New Orleans, where he bought a large ornate mansion in the Uptown district. Today, the house is the residence of the president of Tulane University. Sam the Banana Man acquired a vast amount of wealth from this sale of Cuyamel Fruit Company to United Fruit, and he was also given 300,000 shares of United Fruit stock.

During the Great Depression, however, the United Fruit Company suffered from mismanagement, and stock prices plummeted. In a moment of character-defining acumen, leadership and bravado, Zemurray traveled to Boston, where he confronted the elite members of United Fruit's

The United Fruit Company Building in downtown New Orleans, built in 1920. Today, the building is occupied by Fidelity Homestead Savings Bank. *Photograph by Emily Ford.*

board of directors. When one of the well-to-do directors commented on Zemurray's Russian accent, Zemurray slammed his controlling share of stock on the table and declared with no shortage of English expletives that he would be taking over United Fruit, as they had clearly made enough of a mess of it already. After taking over the company, Zemurray moved its headquarters to New Orleans, where it occupied a building on St. Charles Avenue in the Central Business District. Zemurray lived in the city until his death in 1961. He is remembered as a generous philanthropist who contributed to Tulane University's Middle American Research Institute and donated to Radcliffe University in Massachusetts.

The middle of the twentieth century would be a time of continued inner-metropolitan migration and confrontation for the Jewish community of New Orleans. The movement of established Jews to Uptown continued, as Gates of Prayer relocated to a building at Napoleon Avenue and Coliseum Street in 1920. This trend would continue into the 1970s, when many congregations moved to suburban Metairie.

Congregation Gates of Prayer

January 6, 1850   Re-dedication Service   April 12, 1953

The front cover of a program from the Gates of Prayer synagogue's rededication service. *Congregation Gates of Prayer Manuscript Collection, Louisiana Research Collection, Tulane University.*

Numerous members of the New Orleans Jewish community served in both World War I and II as nurses, soldiers and officers. Leon Godchaux II, the great-grandson of sugar company and department store founder Leon Godchaux, served in the navy during World War II and designed explosives, including a detonator intended for an atomic weapon (although it was never used). Many other daughters, sons, mothers and fathers contributed to the war effort and returned to New Orleans to become inventors, doctors, lawyers and politicians. By 1948, New Orleans was not only home to numerous Jewish veterans of World War II, but it was also home to approximately fifty displaced families who had arrived in the city as survivors of the Holocaust.

The civil rights movement in the 1950s and 1960s brought social tensions across Louisiana and in New Orleans as well. The Jewish community's involvement in New Orleans was significant although, like the approach taken by many southern Jewish communities at the time, mostly low key. Rabbi Max Heller was one exception. Although he died in 1929, the sermons he delivered and activities he organized contributed to the civil rights dialogue. Early in his career at Temple Sinai, he began to equate the unfortunate situation of Eastern European Jewish immigrants with that of African Americans in Louisiana. He compared the anti-Semitic persecution of Alfred Dreyfus in France with the development of Jim Crow laws in Louisiana.

The growing presence of the civil rights movement in New Orleans, however, inspired little participation among the city's Jewish community. Rabbi Julian Feibelman of Temple Sinai was one exception. In 1949, Feibelman opened the temple as an integrated venue for African American political scientist, civil rights supporter and future Nobel Peace Prize winner Ralph Bunche. But across much of the South, Jewish leaders were concerned that public support of desegregation and other civil rights causes would incite violence from civil rights opponents. Between 1954 and 1959, several Jewish institutions were targeted by southern terrorists and bombed. While none of these bombings occurred in New Orleans, the fear of such an event occurring in their city caused Jewish leaders to remain silent while protestors took to the streets and fought for equality. At Gates of Prayer, Rabbi Nathaniel Share, who openly supported desegregation, was asked by the congregation's board to curb his involvement in the movement after the congregation's cemetery was vandalized in 1956.

Those opposed to civil rights legitimized their views using the same early twentieth-century pseudo-scientific explanations for racial inequality that validated anti-Semitism. The first Louisiana branch of the revived Ku Klux Klan had been established in New Orleans in 1920 and was still present in the city by the 1950s. Many southern Jews feared (and understandably so) that public support of activists like the Freedom Riders would draw the attention of racist groups who sought to call Jews "communists" or other incendiary names. In May 1961, George Lincoln Rockwell, the leader of the American Nazi Party and brazen advocate for racial and anti-Semitic violence, traveled to New Orleans in an organized "hate ride" in protest of the Freedom Riders movement. He also planned a protest at the opening of the movie *Exodus* in an attempt to incite the Jewish community. The incident, which forced Holocaust survivors in New Orleans to galvanize against hate together, gave rise to the New Americans Club. From the early 1960s to today, the group of Holocaust survivors and friends conducts remembrance ceremonies at Jewish community centers.

During the 1950s and 1960s, the Jews of New Orleans continued to move farther away from the city's center. The orphanage at St. Charles and Jefferson Avenues was closed and repurposed as a Jewish Community Center. In 1963, the building was demolished, and a new modern building was constructed in its place. The orphans' home organization was reorganized as Jewish Regional Services.

In 1949, Chevra Thilim moved from its Lafayette Avenue synagogue to a location farther uptown. Then, in 1955, as many Orthodox congregations had done at the time, the leaders of Chevra Thilim voted to allow mixed seating in the synagogue, removing the traditional gender-segregated seating arrangement. The decision caused a rift in the congregation and became such an issue that the matter was brought before the Louisiana Supreme Court. The court ruled in favor of the traditionalists, and Chevra Thilim was forced to reinstate divided seating. After the legal battle was over proponents of mixed seating were unsatisfied. Thus, they

The Jewish Community Center located in the Uptown district, New Orleans. *Photograph by Emily Ford.*

left Chevra Thilim to found a Conservative congregation called Tikvat Shalom. In 1978, Tikvat Shalom became one of several congregations to move to suburban Metairie. In 2001, long after Chevra Thilim had permitted mixed seating among its own congregation, the two congregations merged, using Tikvat Shalom's synagogue in suburban Metairie, and adopted the new name Shir Chadash ("New Song").

Beth Israel was one of the first congregations to relocate to the suburbs. The new synagogue, a large modern building at the corner of Canal Boulevard and Walker Street, was open for High Holy Days services in 1970. Gates of Prayer also moved to the suburbs in 1975, and the congregation built a new modern synagogue on West Esplanade Avenue in Metairie. By the mid-1990s, Jews who had made their homes in the far-off exurb of Mandeville, where the causeway terminates on the north side of Lake Pontchartrain, formed the Northshore Jewish Congregation.

CONGREGATION CHEVRA THILIM
חברה תהלים

4429 South Claiborne Ave., 895-7987 & 899-2640 New Orleans, La. 70125

Chevra Thilim letterhead. *Chevra Thilim Collection, Louisiana Research Collection, Tulane University.*

Shir Chadash, New Orleans's Conservative congregation, located in Metairie. *Photograph by Emily Ford.*

Tragically, Beth Israel synagogue suffered significant flooding caused by Hurricanes Katrina and Rita in 2005, which destroyed not only the synagogue but also more than three thousand books, as well as the congregation's seven Torah scrolls, housed inside. In accordance with Jewish

The Gates of Prayer synagogue, Metairie. *Photograph by Emily Ford.*

tradition, the Torah scrolls were given a temporary burial until they could be ceremonially reinterred. In this ceremony, thousands of religious books belonging to Beth Israel and its congregants were also laid to rest. The burial site, located in Beth Israel Cemetery, was designated a monument in 2008.

The widespread flooding and devastation caused by the 2005 hurricanes rocked the entirety of New Orleans, yet the stories of goodwill, charity and mutual aid that have since emerged are provocative and powerful. The response of Touro Infirmary Hospital during Katrina in August 2005 illustrates the great heroics that followed the storm. After the hospital's generators were damaged and could no longer operate, every surviving patient in the hospital was evacuated either by helicopter or by fleets of buses and vans driven by volunteers from outside New Orleans. By September 1, every patient had been evacuated from the hospital. In the coming months, Touro would be the first hospital to reopen its emergency room, and it was the only hospital to provide full care to patients in Orleans Parish until early 2006.

The Beth Israel synagogue at Canal Boulevard and Walker Street, New Orleans. This picture was taken after Hurricane Katrina swept through the area in 2005. *Photograph by Emily Ford.*

Beth Israel was not the only synagogue to receive aid in recovering sacred Torah scrolls; a Chasidic rabbi was also instrumental in securing Torah scrolls from Anshe Sfard. Safely nestled in the Garden District, this synagogue was not flooded, but looting was still a concern. Beth Israel synagogue was the only synagogue in the New Orleans area to be completely destroyed by Hurricane Katrina, but following the storm, the congregation partnered with Gates of Prayer and utilized space at their synagogue on West Esplanade Avenue in Metairie. The two denominations worked together to plan a new synagogue for Beth Israel adjacent to Gates of Prayer. The new synagogue was dedicated on August 24, 2012, nearly seven years after the hurricane's devastation.

The Jewish community of New Orleans remains vibrant and active in the city through such institutions as the Jewish Federation of New Orleans and the Goldring-Woldenburg Institute for Southern Jewish Life, which connects Jewish communities across the southern states. Another New Orleans–based Jewish organization, Chabad of Louisiana, has also aided in community outreach since the 1960s. First established by Rabbi Zelig and Bluma Rivkin and coordinated by the Lubavitcher Rebbe in New York, Rabbi Mendel Schneerson, the state's first Chabad House location was established near Tulane University's campus on Freret Street in 1975. Chabad House continues to provide educational, social and religious programs through the efforts of leaders like David and Nechama Kaufmann; Rabbi Yossie and Chanie Nemes; Rabbi Mendel and Malkie Rivkin; and Rabbi Yochanan and Sara Rivkin. In 1990, Chabad of Louisiana opened another location in Metairie called the Gerson Katz Chabad Center, and the organization has expanded their campus operations to serve Tulane, Loyola and University of New Orleans Jewish students. Additional auxiliary facilities now include the Torah Academy, a school for pre-kindergarten through the eighth grade, and the RINGGER Women's Enrichment Center, which has a *mikvah* (a special bath used for Jewish ritual immersion). In addition to promoting religious programs, Rabbi Yossie Nemes serves as the

Goldring-Woldenberg Jewish Community Campus, Metairie. *Photograph by Emily Ford.*

Right: The Rohr Chabad Jewish Student House. *Photograph by Emily Ford.*

Below: The Kosher Cajun Deli in Metairie. This Jewish New York–style deli serves up sandwiches with a local twist. The deli is under the supervision of the Louisiana Kosher Committee. *Photograph by Emily Ford.*

rabbinic administrator for the Louisiana Kosher Committee (LKC), an organization that works with local restaurants and businesses to provide certified-kosher foods and products.

Recovery efforts in New Orleans continue seven years after Hurricane Katrina devastated the city. The legacy of area Jews, however, remains. Places like the Hermann-Grima House and Judah P. Benjamin's mansion in the French Quarter are still standing, as are many of the synagogue buildings in the city's Uptown and Central City neighborhoods. In addition, the Isidore Newman School and Touro Hospital proudly carry the names of prominent and influential Jews from the city's history, as do many businesses, such as Rubenstein's Department Store and Coleman-Adler Jewelers on Canal Street.

Even more important is the continued contribution of the Jewish community to the culture of New Orleans. This involvement is manifested in various ways, from the almost-daily activities at the Jewish community centers to the yearly conferences at New Orleans's National Center for Black-Jewish Relations, an organization based at Dillard University. It shows itself through the continued reference of various drugstores as "K&B," even though these stores are no more. The slapstick Mardi Gras antics of the Krewe du Jieux have also contributed to the Jewish community; the parade organization's mission is to "co-opt and eradicate" Jewish stereotypes through satire and hilarity. Although the much-publicized refusal of elite Mardi Gras krewes to admit Jewish members must have been influential in the formation of the Krewe du Jieux, the social club's functions go beyond Mardi Gras and include a city-wide Passover seder and an annual Chanukah second-line parade. Another Mardi Gras organization, the Krewe du Mishigas, marches with the famed Krewe du Vieux parade every year. Within New Orleans's grand culinary tradition, one of its lauded restaurants, Dominica, offers a "Passover menu" prepared by chef Alon Shaya. From Stein's Deli on Jackson Street to the Kosher Cajun Deli in Metairie, the continued presence of Jewish culture in New Orleans remains visible and essential.

CHAPTER FIVE

Bayou Towns and the Rise and Decline of Jewish Communities

Few Jews along the Mississippi River suffered losses in the Reconstruction era. As planters returned to their hometowns to find their houses burned, their fields trampled and their slaves emancipated, Jews who were uninvolved in agriculture instead returned to carry on their businesses. In fact, emancipation opened up a new market for those who owned stores, were distributors or were involved in other retail businesses. Many businessmen who were in relatively stable financial positions purchased land parcels that were once part of plantations (which owners divided and sold off after the war to pay off debts).

Profiteers and businessmen nationwide engaged in speculation, sales and trade of all sorts. During the Civil War, Jewish sutlers purchased provisional items from stores and sold them to both Confederate and Union troops. Others acted as brokers, acquiring cotton and other cash crops, which they then sold (both legally and illegally) to buyers. During the war, part of the Union's strategy was to cut the Confederacy off from its overseas trade, particularly the cotton trade with England. This disruption caused a void in the market that welcomed covert financial dealing and opportunism. Leon Haas, like many other Jewish and non-Jewish businessmen, traveled to New York during the war and, from there, transported inventory to New Orleans for sale and utilized the profits to engage in the underground cotton trade that was based in Matamoros and Boca del Rio, Mexico. Peddlers often acted as sutlers themselves, and storekeepers in each town supplied both Union and Confederate forces with in-demand goods.

Although Jews weren't the only ones profiteering during the war, their involvement in wartime commerce fueled anti-Semitism from many sides. The anti-Semitic sentiment that developed among the Confederate states was, according to some historians, part of region-wide prejudice against all foreigners. Jews were also blamed for economic woes that, in reality, sprang from weaknesses in an agrarian system, as it relied heavily on the export of cotton and the import of all other goods. "Anti-Jewish mythology," said Bertram Korn, "had always described the Jew as grasping, thievish, and unscrupulous in business practices; now, in a period of severe economic crisis, the old canard appeared with renewed vigor." During a session of the Confederate legislature, Congressman Henry Foote of Mississippi declared, "Foreign Jews [are] scattered all over the country, under official protection, engaged in trade to the exclusion of our own citizens, undermining our currency." In the town of Talbotton, Georgia, civilians accused Jewish store owners of price gouging and looted the stores while holding proprietors at gunpoint.

The prejudice growing among southerners was troublesome, but the Confederate government did not take any action against Jews. Conversely, Union General Ulysses S. Grant issued Order Number 11, which expelled all Jews—regardless of profession, age, gender or military service—from the Department of Tennessee, a war-division area that included parts of Kentucky and Mississippi. Grant issued the order in December 1862, and it was quickly revoked by President Abraham Lincoln, although not before it had been partly carried out, resulting in arrests and forced removals of a small number of Jews in the northern Mississippi towns of Holly Springs and Oxford.

Despite the discrimination Jewish Southerners faced, many prospered, including Jacob Lemann and Abraham Klotz, both of whom were from Donaldsonville, and Leon Godchaux, who, by that time, was living in New Orleans. After serving the Confederacy during the war, Klotz returned to Donaldsonville and acquired two plantations, which came to be known as Star and Klotzville Plantations. Situated along

Bayou Lafourche and just upriver from the town of Thibodeaux, both plantations are in unincorporated townships today. It wasn't common for Jews to become planters after the war, but those who did, in the words of Elliot Ashkenazi, "applied the capitalist practices of the merchant, not those of the feudal baron, to the running of plantations." Klotz, like Godchaux and Lemann, sought to minimize supply costs in his sugar operations by acquiring refineries and taking advantage of rail lines and river routes between his plantations.

Although some sources claim Leon Godchaux entered the sugar business prior to the Civil War, it is unclear exactly when he purchased Reserve Plantation, which is located along the Mississippi River between New Orleans and Donaldsonville. By 1869, however, the plantation was in his possession, and he was already acquiring additional properties. Over the next thirty years before his death, Godchaux would become the "sugar king" of Louisiana, a title he would pass on to his children and other members of his family who continued the business. In all, Godchaux owned fourteen plantations, including Diamond, LaPlace, LaBranche, Belle Point and New Era Plantations near Reserve, as well as plantations near Napoleonville and Raceland, Louisiana. Some of these plantation houses are still standing. Diamond Plantation, which was at different times known as Trepagnier Plantation and Myrtle Land Plantation, was sold in the 1920s to the U.S. Army Corps of Engineers, which built the Bonne Carré Spillway, a flood control system built in the aftermath of the Great Flood of 1927.

Godchaux streamlined his plantations' operations and distribution of product by utilizing local resources and financial savvy. Beginning in the 1890s, he constructed a narrow-gauge rail line that connected some of his plantations. In the first years of his business, he used a mule team to pull sugar cane on carts along the rail but replaced it with steam-powered locomotive once it was introduced in 1895. He built three refineries to operate on-site at his plantations, which not only limited his expenses in the refining process but also allowed him to charge other nearby sugar operations for use of the refineries. The Godchaux steam engines, which by the 1930s were painted with the Godchaux name on them, connected with the Yazoo & Mississippi Rail Line, which allowed

A steam-engine locomotive in Reserve, Louisiana, once used by the Godchaux Sugar Company. *Photograph by Emily Ford.*

The Godchaux Sugar Refinery in Reserve, Louisiana. *Library of Congress Prints and Photographs Division.*

Godchaux to easily transport his product across the South. By 1904, Godchaux Sugar's refineries were producing nearly twenty-five thousand tons of sugar per year and employed as many as two thousand people on its various plantations. Godchaux Sugar remained a household name in Louisiana until 1958, when the company was sold to the National Sugar and Refining Company.

Jacob Lemann returned to Donaldsonville in 1864. The town by that time had suffered wartime devastation and was under Union control. Because he had been in New York and Europe during the war, he was not affected by the Confiscation Acts, which allowed the Federal government to seize the land of those who supported insurrection. Some planters, many of whom owed Lemann money for credit transactions they made prior to the war, died in battle. Over the next thirty years, Lemann would establish a network of sugar cane plantations and sell the sugar produced in his Donaldsonville store. He also paid his workers, which was uncommon through much of the South, as sharecropping—a system where workers grew crops and surrendered a share of their yield to landowners at the end of a season—was the dominant agricultural system following the Civil War. Lemann's interests were managed in such a way that his plantation employees, who were predominantly freed African Americans, were sure to spend their wages at Lemann's store but, as opposed to sharecropping, they were less likely to accrue debilitating debt to him.

Jacob Lemann's store was built in 1877 at the corner of Mississippi and Railroad Streets in Donaldsonville. His sons Bernard and Mayer Lemann assumed control over the business in the late nineteenth century and continued to partner with numerous Jewish suppliers and merchants in New Orleans. B. Lemann & Bro. not only provided numerous plantations in the area with the necessary tools and supplies to farm but also acted as the primary department and general store in Donaldsonville and sold everything from hardware and clothing to liquor and groceries.

Klotz, Godchaux and Lemann were not the only Jews who saw their businesses prosper during the Reconstruction era, but they were among the most unique in the breadth and nature of their success. The Lemanns' store was particularly exceptional. When the store finally closed in the

An invoice from Frank, Haas & Company, a dry-goods store in New Orleans, signed by Bernard Lemann on September 17, 1872. The invoice is evidence of the Lemann family's financial interests in Louisiana during Reconstruction. *Lemann Family Papers, Louisiana Research Collection, Tulane University.*

early 1980s, it was the oldest continuously operated department store in the state. Today, it houses the Historic Donaldsonville Museum.

Each town along the Mississippi River experienced its own process of rebuilding and community development. The extent of the damage incurred from the war varied from town to town. Vicksburg was devastated as a result of Union attacks on the city, and the town of Grand Gulf was barely standing by the time Union forces defeated Confederates. Stores in Port Gibson, as well as those in other towns, were looted, and property was stolen, but in a decision that has become legendary to the present day, Grant declared Port Gibson "too beautiful to burn" and continued upriver.

Congregations that had been established before the war expanded and matured in the second half of the nineteenth century. Plaquemine's Hebrew Benevolent Society reorganized as congregation Ohavai Shalom ("Lovers of Peace") in 1878 and continued to utilize their building near the Mississippi River for services. Temple Sinai was built in St. Francisville in 1901 and was the first and only synagogue in the town. The Hebrew Congregation of Baton Rouge reorganized in 1868 as Shaare Chesed and then again in 1885 as B'nai Israel. A complicated set of events caused the congregation to move from its first building to another in 1877, but it then moved back to its original building in 1883, where it remained until a new synagogue was constructed in the mid-twentieth century. Between 1865 and 1900, Jewish communities in Vicksburg, Port Gibson, Natchez, Woodville and Donaldsonville would all establish purpose-built synagogues.

The old Temple B'nai Israel of Baton Rouge, Louisiana. *William A. Rosenthall Judaica Collection, Special Collections, College of Charleston.*

Vicksburg's Anshe Chesed congregation constructed the state's first purpose-built synagogue in 1870. The imposing brick building on Cherry Street between China and Clay Streets was originally constructed in the Gothic style but was remodeled in 1893 and given a Romanesque façade. When it was dedicated in May 1870, the congregation held a grand dedication ball on the steamer *Paragoud.* In 1862, the congregation consisted of roughly fifty families. The construction of the synagogue and the grand ball that followed is indicative of the unity that characterized the Jewish community at the time, as well as how prominent its members were in Vicksburg society.

After purchasing a lot for the new synagogue in 1868, the congregation of Vicksburg began the search for an ordained rabbi to lead them. Bavarian immigrant Bernard Henry Gotthelf, who was a chazzan in Louisville, Kentucky, at the time, leapt at the opportunity. Gotthelf was born in 1819 and came to America with his wife in 1841. He served as the second Jewish chaplain for the Union forces during the Civil War and relocated to Vicksburg in 1867 to take the position of rabbi for Anshe Chesed. He led the congregation until his death in 1878. Gotthelf was one of many in Vicksburg who died in that year's yellow fever epidemic.

Left: The Anshe Chesed synagogue, Vickburg, Mississippi, built in 1870. *William A. Rosenthall Judaica Collection, Special Collections, College of Charleston.*

Below: Photograph of a wedding inside the Anshe Chesed synagogue, Vickburg, Mississippi. *Goldring-Woldenberg Institute of Southern Jewish Life.*

The disease claimed the lives of ten other members of the congregation, including Gotthelf's twenty-year-old son. Rabbi Herman Bien, known to congregants as the "Poet Rabbi" for his literary skills, succeeded Gotthelf. He did not serve Anshe Chesed long, however, and after leaving Vicksburg, he committed suicide in 1895. Anshe Chesed was then led by Rabbi George Solomon, a recent graduate of Hebrew Union College in Cincinnati who headed the congregation until 1903.

Natchez's B'nai Israel congregation, formerly Chevra Kedusha, completed its synagogue building in 1872. The Greek Revival building, which bore quoins on its edges and had a projecting pediment and portico, was destroyed by fire in 1903. Luckily, the rabbi's residence next door was not destroyed. The residence, known as the Parsonage, still stands today. The congregation organized and planned the synagogue's rebuilding a few days following the disaster and used the Jefferson Street Methodist Church as a temporary house of worship in the meantime. The building, constructed in the Beaux-Arts style, was completed in 1905 and was dedicated in a service led by Isaac Mayer Wise at 213 Commerce Street.

The B'nai Israel synagogue, Natchez, Mississippi. The synagogue was built by architect Harry Overbeck in 1905. *William A. Rosenthall Judaica Collection, Special Collections, College of Charleston.*

Services at the Dedication *of*

Temple B'nai Israel,

Natchez, Miss.

March 24th--25th,   2nd Adar 17th--18th,
1905.   5665.

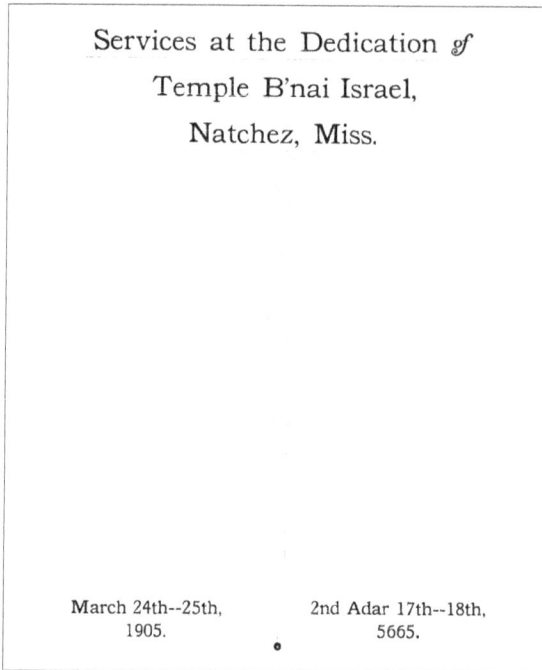

A dedication program booklet for the B'nai Israel synagogue in Natchez, Mississippi. *Rabbi Jacob S. Raisin Papers, Special Collections, College of Charleston.*

A handsome structure with delicately ornamented columns, a projecting portico and immense transom light, the new synagogue fit in perfectly with Natchez's plantation houses and grandiose mansions. The building's design was so handsome that a nearly identical building was designed for Hebrew Union congregation in Meridian, Mississippi, the very next year.

Both B'nai Israel in Natchez and Anshe Chesed in Vicksburg joined the Reform movement in the early 1870s and were early members of the Union of American Hebrew Congregations. Samuel Ullman, who had moved to Natchez in 1865 from Woodville after his service in the Confederacy, joined Isaac Lowenburg, Henry Frank, John Mayer, Joseph Levy, Philip Wexler and Charles Katz in pushing for the change. John Mayer's wife, Jannette, was particularly passionate about Reform, and according to Sam Ullman, she worried that "the children were growing up like heathen [*sic*]" and suggested the need for a Sunday school. Ullman started the Sunday school program with the help of the Mayers' daughter Emma, whom he married two years later. Isaac Lowenburg was also dedicated to the development of B'nai Israel. In 1870, he traveled to

Hechingen, Germany, and returned with a Torah scroll for the synagogue that he received from a German congregation. The congregation was led by Rabbi Emanuel M. Rosenfelder, who had previously served at Beth Israel in Woodville in 1876.

In Donaldsonville, Bikur Cholim completed its synagogue in 1871. The large wooden structure originally had a high portico with lace-like wooden embellishments. (The portico was removed in the mid-twentieth century to adapt the building for use as a hardware store.) Bikur Cholim did not join the Reform movement until 1901. During the Reconstruction era, Donaldsonville was home not only to sugar giants like Jacob Lemann and Abraham Klotz but also additional sugar cane planters like Melville Israel, who owned land outside Donaldsonville, and merchants like Samuel Blum, Henry Pforzheimer and Maas Tobias. A few Jews in Donaldsonville, like Isaac Lowenburg, who became mayor

The Bikur Cholim synagogue in Donaldsonville, Louisiana, built in 1871. After the congregation folded in the 1950s, the building was converted into a hardware store. *Photograph by Emily Ford.*

of Natchez, and Benjamin Franklin Jonas, one of Louisiana's senators, became involved in politics during the Reconstruction period. Other Jews worked on a local level, serving as aldermen and mayors, as well as other positions.

Two Jewish politicians in Donaldsonville became rivals in a very peculiar—and significant—incident, which was reflective of greater trends in Reconstruction Louisiana. Marx Schoenburg, who was born in the German province of Hesse-Kassel in 1833, immigrated to Ohio around 1852 and then made his way to New Orleans in 1855. He moved to Donaldsonville in 1868 with his new wife, whose sister lived there with her husband, Morris Marks. Both Marks and Schoenburg were Republicans, which, at that time, equated to a general affiliation with Union interests and politics. It was also the party that most African Americans belonged to. Louisiana during the Reconstruction years was a battleground of competing Republicans and southern Democrats, and oftentimes, this resulted in political conflict at the local and state levels. In 1870, Henry Warmoth, the Republican governor of Louisiana, appointed Marx Schoenburg as mayor of Donaldsonville and Morris Marks as a judge in Ascension Parish. Both appointments were likely the result of political favoritism and were met with hostility among the white Democrats of Donaldsonville. To make matters worse, another man, Democrat William C. Lawes, had already been elected as mayor of Donaldsonville before Schoenburg's appointment. The matter was finally brought before Judge Morris Marks, who declared that Schoenburg was not the town's legitimate mayor and declared Lawes the rightful officeholder.

During the election of 1870, political tensions culminated in a power grab from all sides. Morris Marks and members of a local Republican militia seized the Donaldsonville ballot boxes, claiming that they were preventing inevitable voter fraud (though it's possible they intended to commit fraud themselves). The militia clashed with Democrat and radical Republican forces, resulting in violence. In the mêlée that followed, Schoenburg was shot in the chest and killed. Newspaper accounts covering the incident varied. One claimed he was shot by William Lawes, whom he was reportedly working with to preserve the peace of Donaldsonville. Another claimed that an angry mob of African Americans shot him because they saw him as a protector of white interests. And still another article reported that his death had been an accident. The incident became a telling event in the story of Reconstruction in Louisiana, as it reflected the competing interests and rising tension in small-town communities.

During the 1860s, the Beth Israel congregation of Woodville, Mississippi, established the Woodville Hebrew Education Association and built a synagogue in 1878. The large wooden building was embellished with colorful panels and was flanked with a tower on each side of the primary façade. The wooden, gable-roofed Beth Israel building was also accented with two large tablets on the face of its pediment reminiscent of New Orleans's early Gates of Mercy synagogue and countless other synagogues designed by Emile Weil. The synagogue served "Little Jerusalem" (as the community called itself) as it continued to grow in the years following the Civil War.

Isaac Hart, a prominent member of Woodville's Jewish community and a realtor, helped to procure a suitable rabbi for Beth Israel after Rabbi Emanuel Rosenfelder left to serve Natchez's B'nai Israel. Hart's

The Beth Israel synagogue of Woodville, Mississippi, built in 1878. In the 1920s, the congregation disbanded, and the building was renovated into a movie theater, which was destroyed by fire in the 1930s. *Library of Congress Prints and Photographs Division.*

first choice was the young Rabbi Henry Cohen. Born in London in a year when many members of his Woodville congregation were fighting for the Confederacy, Rabbi Cohen was a translator in Africa and a rabbi in Jamaica before he arrived in Mississippi in 1885, at the age of twenty-two. The young rabbi was described as a gripping orator who captivated his congregation for three years before he transferred to a congregation in Galveston, Texas. His charisma as a speaker and as a rabbi actually briefly helped quell an ongoing dilemma among Jewish businessmen in small southern towns.

Observance of the Jewish Sabbath remained a point of contention among Jews in the South and across the United States during the nineteenth and twentieth centuries. While Woodville was not the only venue for this debate (New Orleans Jews were active in the argument surrounding the city's Sunday closure laws in the 1890s), the town was a typical Mississippi River town in that it was primarily composed of Jewish merchants and Christian farmers and planters. It was traditional for farmers to travel into town to purchase supplies and visit friends on Saturday, the Jewish Sabbath, in order to ensure their observance of the Christian day of rest, which is on Sunday. In order to accommodate their Christian customers and keep their business, Jewish merchants in Woodville kept their stores open on Saturday. Rabbi Henry Cohen, however, compelled these merchants to compromise. He suggested that Jewish businessmen only keep their stores open on Saturday afternoons so that they could attend Beth Israel's Saturday morning service. It is worth noting that Rabbi Cohen's services were so entertaining that Christian planters who traveled to town on Saturdays would often attend Beth Israel's services in order to hear him themselves.

A number of Jewish civic and fraternal organizations sprung up in the communities along the lower Mississippi River due in part to the increased activity of existing congregations and the establishment of new ones. Benevolent societies, ladies' aid groups, Hebrew and religious schools, branches of B'nai B'rith and other organizations were developed in practically every town that had a synagogue. In Vicksburg, the Young Men's Hebrew Benevolent Association was formed in 1871 and changed its name to the B'nai B'rith Literary Stock Company in 1886. The "B.B.

The B'nai B'rith Club building in Vicksburg, Mississippi. *Photograph by Emily Ford.*

Club," as it came to be known, erected a building on the corner of Clay and Walnut Streets in the 1890s to use as its headquarters. The building eventually housed the city's first indoor swimming pool. Sadly, it burned in 1915, but it was quickly replaced with a newer building that was more elegant and also somewhat eclectic in style. The new building also featured an immense library and upstairs ballroom and was used by the Anshe Chesed congregation for social gatherings.

Plaquemine, Louisiana, had a healthy Jewish community that was supported by Congregation Ohavai Shalom, and it also had a rich civic and commercial life. A number of Jews migrated to the town during Reconstruction and opened businesses, mostly dry-goods and clothing stores, many of which prospered from railroad and river commerce. Yet like Rodney and Grand Gulf before it, Plaquemine fell victim to the fickle Mississippi River in 1880. The river changed route, as it often did in the years before engineered levees and flood control projects, and in its shift, the river consumed a portion of the town, including the congregation's synagogue. The building fell into the river, along with numerous Jewish-owned businesses. The congregation, which numbered around sixty people in the 1870s, recovered slowly, and after twenty-five years, it constructed a new house of worship. By that time, approximately fifteen families reorganized Ohavai Shalom and established a Hebrew school in Plaquemine as well. Ohavai Shalom's new synagogue was located on Eden Street, three blocks inland from the river's edge.

The last half of the nineteenth century brought forth an enormous wave of Jewish immigrants from Eastern Europe, most of whom were from Russia, Hungary, Romania and Poland. Like those before them, these immigrants fled Europe in order to escape persecution. Yet while the Jews of France, Germany and Alsace-Lorraine were emancipated and recognized as citizens in the late nineteenth and early twentieth centuries, such relief from segregation and disenfranchisement did not occur in the Russian Empire, where most Jews were forced to live in ghettos with little room to expand beyond poverty. In Eastern Europe, under Czar Alexander III, more laws that restricted the rights of Jews were passed, and anti-Semitism led to bloody pogroms, starvation and death. The population movement out of Eastern Europe from the early 1880s to the beginning of World War I was so vast that numerous immigrant-aid societies in Europe and the United States were organized to support impoverished newcomers. Entire villages uprooted and relocated to New York and other port cities, which created a cultural influx. Many of these immigrants, unlike those from previous waves, did not quickly assimilate into American society.

In New Orleans, the Immigrants' Aid Association was headed by Julius Weis. In 1881, the Immigrants' Aid Association, along with the Hebrew Emigrant Aid Association of New York, organized a massive effort to fund an agricultural colony in Sicily Island, Louisiana, a settlement in Catahoula Parish that was just up the river from Baton Rouge. Herman Rosenthall, who was part of the *Am Olam* or "Eternal People" movement, planned the colony to be an agricultural village where its "colonists" could farm, maintain their religious traditions and live in prosperity. Sicily Island was the first Jewish agricultural colony in the United States, although many more would follow. After arriving in New Orleans and gathering provisions—including building materials, harnesses, plows and seeds—with the help of the Immigrants' Aid Association, the roughly fifty male colonists traveled upriver to their homestead, which had been sold to them by Isidore and Henry Newman. Once the men finished building their homes, their families were allowed to join them.

The colonists settled in Sicily Island in the winter of 1882 but soon found that the land was poorly suited for farming. Even though some colonists had experience in agriculture and trade (the original report on the colony lists eleven farmers, a saddler and a tinsmith), the colony failed to produce enough to survive. Further calamities ensued, the most deadly of which was a malaria outbreak. Finally, a flood on the river wiped out the colonists' houses and depleted their livestock. The colony was abandoned in 1883, although some colonists followed Herman Rosenthall to his next utopian experiment in Cremieux, South Dakota. The Cremieux settlement also failed and was disbanded in 1889 after a number of natural disasters.

The new Eastern European Jewish immigrants to Vicksburg quickly found discomfort with the Reform doctrine of Anshe Chesed and, although they were a small group, formed an Orthodox congregation known as Ahavas Achim in 1900. The new traditionalist congregation met at the old Masonic Hall in Vicksburg, but it never acquired the services of a rabbi. The division between the established, mostly German Jews and the Russian, Hungarian and Romanian Jews who had arrived in Vicksburg troubled the members of Anshe Chesed, who reasoned that the community as a whole was not large enough to warrant two congregations of two separate branches of Judaism. In the next few years, Rabbi Sol Kory, who served Anshe Chesed from 1903 to 1936, made great efforts to accommodate the Orthodox Jews, enough so that they rejoined the Reform synagogue.

Although Jews had lived in Bayou Sara and St. Francisville since the antebellum period, it wasn't until the late nineteenth century that

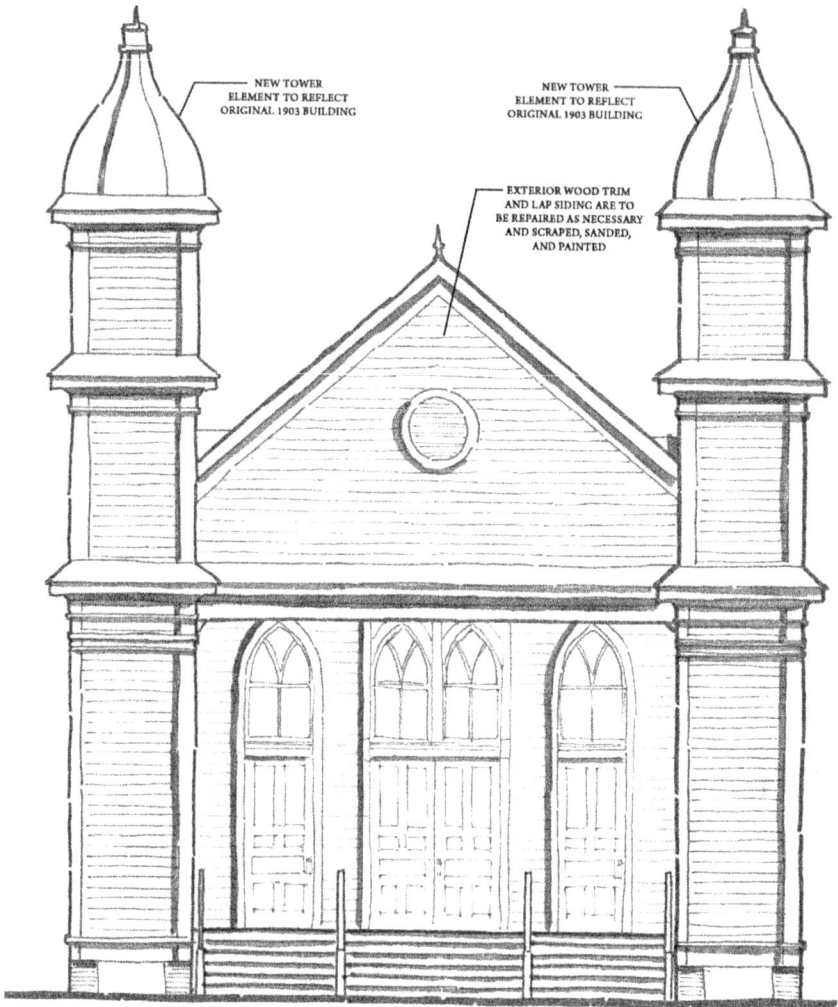

WEST ELEVATION (TEMPLE SINAI)

Plans for the restoration of Temple Sinai, St. Francisville, Louisiana. Historic photographs have revealed that the original building had two towers on its front façade. *Holly and Smith Architects, APAC.*

a number of prominent members of the community established religious institutions. In 1891, dry-goods store owner, cotton merchant and broker Julius Freyhan purchased land for use as a Jewish cemetery in St. Francisville. Shortly thereafter, grocer, banker and livery stable owner Adolph Teutsch led a committee to establish a synagogue in St. Francisville. The congregation developed slowly over the next ten years, and in 1903, Temple Sinai, a handsome wooden building with a gable roof and two towers on its flanks, was completed on Prosperity Street. Benjamin Mann, who, like Teutsch, also owned a livery stable, helped to formally organize the congregation in 1901. When Temple Sinai was opened, both Jews and non-Jews attended the dedication.

Julius Freyhan was a prominent figure in West Feliciana Parish and had a wide array of interests. He ran a mercantile store but was also a real estate investor. Like Jacob Lemann and numerous other Jewish merchants in the agricultural South, he supplied farmers with goods and equipment. In his obituary, he was lauded for extending credit to his customers in times of poor crop yield and low market prices. He acted as a cotton broker as well, and his success led him to New Orleans in the 1880s, where he took over Lane Cotton Mills, the leading cotton company in the state. His company also managed accounts for sharecropping operations like Oakley Plantation near St. Francisville, which was the antebellum home of John James Audubon.

Despite relocating to New Orleans, Julius Freyhan maintained business interests and civic ties in St. Francisville, where he owned a number of stores, an opera house and a saloon. He also had private residences in both St. Francisville and Bayou Sara. Freyhan, like many of his contemporaries, was also a great philanthropist. He donated an organ to St. Francisville's Temple Sinai, and his wife, Sarah, participated in the St. Francisville Ladies' Aid Society. Much like Judah Touro, Freyhan's greatest gesture came to the town of St. Francisville through his last will and testament. Freyhan died in 1904 after suffering a stroke and left $8,000 toward the building of St. Francisville's first public school. His wife orchestrated the establishment of the building, and in 1905, the two-and-one-half-story brick Julius Freyhan School was opened. Tragically, the new school was destroyed by fire in 1907 but was reconstructed the next year and served the town as an education center for another forty years.

The late nineteenth century proved to be halcyon days for the Jewish communities along the Mississippi River. While they remained small, the prominence and success of their members grew by leaps and bounds.

Towns like Natchez, Vicksburg, Woodville and Donaldsonville featured handsome synagogues and gorgeous homes that belonged to the towns' most well-to-do families. However, the Jewish populations among these towns slowly began to decline. With few exceptions, the Jewish communities of the Mississippi River would all but disappear by the mid-twentieth century. The sons and daughters of immigrants, who grew up in relatively greater stability, comfort and opportunity than their parents, looked for opportunities outside their hometowns; many attended out-of-state colleges while others moved to cities to find employment. Others went on to marry into Jewish families in New Orleans, St. Louis, Memphis and other cities. In addition, the early twentieth-century impact of the destructive boll weevil depleted the cotton economies of Louisiana and Mississippi. This caused Jewish businesses that brokered in cotton and supplied cotton farmers to either move to New Orleans in order to serve a larger market or close their enterprises entirely. Finally, various incidents of "whitecapping"— lawless vigilantism that sought to harm Jewish businesses for employing African Americans—occurred in Lake Providence and Delhi, Louisiana and alarmed many of the Jews living within the state. Many relocated to New Orleans to protect themselves and their families.

The lynching of Leo M. Frank in Marietta, Georgia, in 1915 was the most troubling manifestation of growing nativism and anti-Semitism in the South. Also, the willingness of Jewish businesses to serve African Americans caused ire among members of the reformed Ku Klux Klan, as well as others who sought an explanation for the sad economic state of the South in the early twentieth century. Yet despite this pressure to participate in the politics of segregation, Jewish businesses within the delta region continued to serve African Americans as they would any other customer. In Natchez, Rabbis Isaac Mayer Wise and Seymour Bottigheimer arranged for George Washington Carver, the renowned African American scientist and inventor, to speak at B'nai Israel synagogue. Yet the changing social and economic climates of Mississippi and Louisiana, in conjunction with the growing preference of young people to live in greater urban centers, caused Jews to move away from their small riverside communities. The economic effects of the Great Depression also made small-town living more difficult.

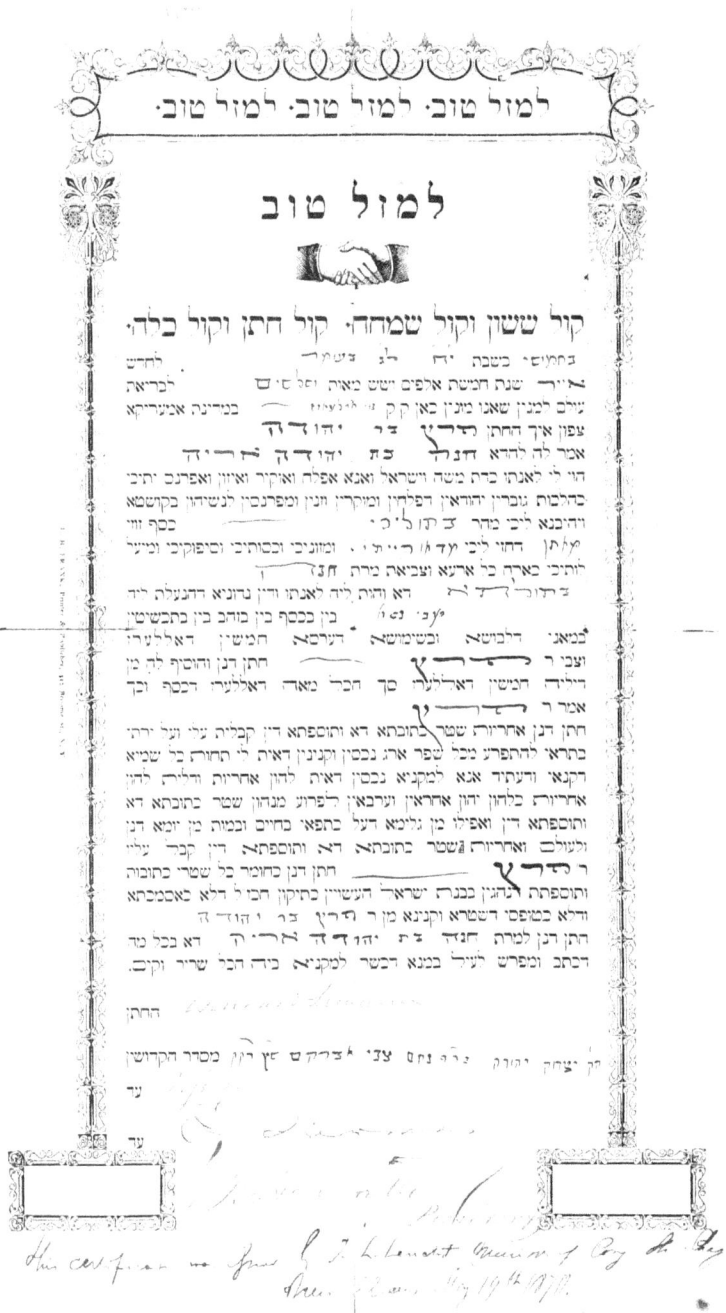

The *ketubah* (Hebrew marriage certificate) of Bernard Lemann of Donaldsonville and Harriet Friedheim of New Orleans, dated May 19, 1870. This documents one of many instances where a small-town boy married a big-city girl. *Lemann Family Papers, Louisiana Research Collection, Tulane University.*

In the 1890s, Donaldsonville's Bikur Cholim congregation reorganized to suit its dwindling numbers. By 1919, the congregation's population hovered around one hundred and, over the next thirty years, continued to decline. By 1954, Bikur Cholim had disbanded, and the next year, the synagogue was sold. Although there were, in addition to racial tension and anti-Semitism, many other factors that contributed to Jewish migration from the delta, the town of Donaldsonville was particularly affected by intermarriage. The population of Ascension Parish was largely French Acadian and Catholic. Many Jews who lived in the area, such as Jacob Lemann, married local women but did not convert to Catholicism. But by the end of the twentieth century, only two Jews remained in Donaldsonville—Gaston Hirsch and Irv Birnbaum. Hirsch, a French World War II veteran, moved to Donaldsonville in the late 1940s and was the caretaker of Bikur Sholim Cemetery. He was, for years, considered the "Last Jew in Donaldsonville." Before his death in 1994, Hirsch arranged for three men to tend to the cemetery after his death. All three were Christians by faith, but each had one Jewish parent. Irv Birnbaum moved to Donaldsonville in the 1980s. A former haberdasher for Kohn-Turner in New York, he also tended to Bikur Sholim Cemetery until his death in 2004.

Urbanization took many Jews from Plaquemine. Ohavai Shalom attempted to reorganize in the early twentieth century, but the town was so close to the growing capital of Baton Rouge that families eventually began taking the ferry to the city to attend B'nai Israel. By 1932, the congregation closed its doors, and most Jews relocated to Baton Rouge or elsewhere. The town of Baton Rouge and its Jewish community thrived throughout the twentieth century.

Baton Rouge was also the new site of one of the most stunning architectural pieces created by a Jewish firm. The Louisiana State Capitol, which was designed by the New Orleans architectural firm Weiss, Dreyfous, and Seiferth, was completed in 1932. The firm would go on to design numerous buildings across the state of Louisiana, including the governor's mansion in Baton Rouge, the Jung Hotel and Charity Hospital in New Orleans, the Eola Hotel in Natchez and the administration building serving New Orleans's Huey Long Bridge. But the capitol building remains the firm's crowning achievement. In fact, it is

The Louisiana State Capitol in Baton Rouge, designed and built by New Orleans architectural firm Weiss, Dreyfous, and Seiferth in 1932. *Photograph by Emily Ford.*

the tallest capitol building in the United States and bears handsome carvings from its steps to its apex.

The city's B'nai Israel synagogue became the venue for a community disagreement present among Jewish congregations nationwide. In 1885, the Reform movement established the Pittsburgh Platform, which outlined the standards of Reform Judaism. Among its various tenets was the denomination's rejection of *kashrut*, as well as other rituals. Reformist Jews notably disagreed with Zionists, who support the establishment of a Jewish state. Yet by the end of World War II, Reform congregations had begun to support the creation of a Jewish homeland, and many congregants remained opposed. A congregation in Houston, Texas, added an anti-Zionist clause its constitution, and the B'nai Israel congregation in Baton Rouge did the same in 1945. Many members of B'nai Israel did not support this action and subsequently broke away from the congregation. These former members gathered in 1945 and organized

LIBERAL SYNAGOGUE
260 Oakwood, Corner Willshire
BATON ROUGE 12, LA.

MARVIN M. REZNIKOFF, Rabbi

The Liberal synagogue of Baton Rouge, Louisiana, as depicted on the congregation's stationery. The synagogue is now called Beth Shalom. *Chevra Thilim Collection, Louisiana Research Collection, Tulane University.*

B'nai Israel's current synagogue in Baton Rouge, Louisiana. *Photograph by Emily Ford.*

a new congregation called the Liberal synagogue, which would later be renamed Beth Shalom. Both B'nai Israel and Beth Shalom continue to serve the Jewish community today, although both have relatively small memberships. Additionally, both provided vast amounts of aid to New Orleans's Jewish community following Hurricane Katrina and continued to provide community assistance through the subsequent ravages of Hurricane Rita.

One of the most visible legacies of Baton Rouge's Jewish community was, until the late 1990s, Goudchaux's Department Store, established by Bernard and Jacob Goudchaux in 1907. In 1939, the store was purchased by Erich Sternberg, an emigrant from Germany who, along with his wife Lea, fled Europe to escape the growing threat of Nazism. Sternberg kept the store name and, with the help of his wife and children, began a business that would thrive over the next six decades. In the 1980s, the Sternberg family purchased the Maison Blanche Building on Canal Street in New Orleans and renamed the store Maison Blanche Department Store. The building was built in the 1910s by Isidore Newman to replace the original Maison Blanche building that was demolished in 1908. Maison Blanche remained part of the Goudchaux Department Store Company until 1992, when it was sold to Dillard's. Goudchaux's main store in Baton Rouge closed when the company went bankrupt in the late 1990s. Today, the old building retains decorative elements from the Goudchaux period, including attractive tile signage and modern-style porticos.

The Jewish community in St. Francisville began to decline long before the 1940s Reform/Zionist controversy. As many Jews followed Julius Freyhan's lead and moved to larger cities like New Orleans, the membership of Temple Sinai slowly dwindled. Over the course of two decades, the congregation was served by a series of rabbis who visited from elsewhere, including Max Heller of New Orleans, Marx Klein of Donaldsonville and Max Raisin, who had previously served congregation Gemiluth Chassed in Port Gibson. In 1921, the synagogue was sold to the St. Francisville Presbyterian Church, and by the early 1940s, the congregation was all but disbanded.

Woodville was one of many towns in Mississippi and Louisiana that were devastated by the invasion of the boll weevil. The low cotton yields eventually prompted members of the Jewish community to seek greener pastures elsewhere. Woodville's Beth Israel synagogue, like St. Francisville's Temple Sinai, was sold in the 1920s. Unlike St. Francisville's Temple Sinai, however, Beth Israel synagogue was moved across town and eventually repurposed as a movie theater until it burned down in 1935.

While Woodville and St. Francisville retained their small-town status, the town of Natchez grew, and for a time, so did its Jewish population. B'nai Israel continued to serve the Natchez Jewish community, and Jewish businesses continued to thrive. Many extended members of the Geisenberger, Frank, Lowenburg and Mayer families continued to live and do business in the city. The Levy family, which had members in both Natchez and New Orleans, commissioned Weiss, Dreyfous and Seiferth to design the imposing Eola Hotel in downtown Natchez in the late 1920s (the family later sold the property). The drive to relocate, as well as intermarriage between Jews and non-Jews, eventually took its toll on the city's Jewish population, and it gradually declined to only a handful of people today.

Port Gibson had much more in common with the little towns of Woodville and St. Francisville in the twentieth century than it did with Natchez. Claiborne County as a whole experienced a decline in population between 1910 and 1920 as more people moved to nearby

Port Gibson's Gemiluth Chassed synagogue, built in 1892. The synagogue was used by the congregation until 1986. Today, the building is a designated landmark. *Rabbi Jacob S. Raisin Papers, Special Collections, College of Charleston.*

cities; the Jewish population suffered the most drastic decline—a net loss of 53 percent. A number of Jewish-owned businesses in Port Gibson closed, and Gemiluth Chassed could no longer support the services of a full-time rabbi after 1908. Felix Bock, who was fluent in Hebrew, led the town's small congregation until his death in 1933. Services were held inconsistently over the next few years, and in 1986, the beautiful synagogue with its onion domes and keyhole windows was sold to the Lum family, non-Jewish preservationists who sought to save the landmark building.

In 1969, Vicksburg's Anshe Chesed congregation abandoned its synagogue building on Cherry Street. Negotiations with the National Park Service, which managed Vicksburg National Military Park, resulted in a "land-swap," in which Anshe Chesed was given land directly beside the congregation's historic cemetery. In the late 1960s, a new temple was built at the new location, and though it was farther outside downtown

The new Anshe Chesed synagogue, located near the Vicksburg National Military Park. *Photograph by Emily Ford.*

Vicksburg and somewhat smaller, it reflected the changes that were occurring among the congregation. Just as in Natchez, Vicksburg's Jewish population slowly declined as its younger generation moved away and its older members continued to age. Today, Anshe Chesed maintains regular services among the dozen or so members who remain in Vicksburg. Although small in number, the congregation remains tenacious, meeting each week to share services and meals.

Although the Jewish communities that were once present in so many of Louisiana and Mississippi's riverside towns have all but vanished, they have definitely left their mark. Structures that once served as homes, businesses or places of worship remain, each with its own story to tell. Fading signs on building walls still direct the traveler to Goudchaux's Department Store in Baton Rouge, and in Vicksburg, the beautifully restored B.B. Club now serves as an event venue. In the cemeteries of St. Francisville, Natchez and Woodville, stones delicately etched with outstretched Cohenim hands and the names of Jewish immigrants stand as silent witnesses to an abundant heritage. But they are not alone. On many headstones one can find small pebbles, traditional tokens of remembrance and a sign that someone was there. That the pebbles remain and continue to grow in number is only one small reminder that the legacy of Louisiana and Mississippi Jews is carefully tended.

⁂ftㅐerword

As Jewish communities in the Mississippi River delta continue to decline, special interest groups have formed with the mission of preserving not only the material legacy of southern Jewish communities but also their history and culture. The Museum of the Southern Jewish Experience (MSJE) was established in 1986 and has since worked to collect and preserve artifacts from small towns along the lower Mississippi River that tell the story of the southern Jewish communities and the dynamic presence they once had in this region. In 1991, MSJE entered into a partnership with the remaining members of B'nai Israel, guaranteeing the preservation as a museum of Natchez Jewish history when it is no longer in use as a place of worship. In 2000, MSJE expanded its mission to include educational and rabbinic services for small communities that still retain a strong Jewish identity. That same year, the museum was renamed the Goldring-Woldenberg Institute for Southern Jewish Life (ISJL), and it continues to be a steward of southern Jewish heritage.

Efforts to preserve Jewish history and culture in Louisiana and Mississippi are also active in other localities. The town of St. Francisville and the Freyhan Foundation have also worked to restore both the Julius Freyhan School and Temple Sinai building and repurpose them as preservation centerpieces. Working closely with the Jewish community in New Orleans and elsewhere, the ISJL has also succeeded in obtaining some federal

The historical marker at B'nai Israel in Natchez, Mississippi, erected by the Institute for Southern Jewish Life and the Jewish American Society for Historic Preservation. *Photograph by Emily Ford.*

preservation funding and has begun work on Temple Sinai. Although no Jews live in St. Francisville today, the preservation of the legacy of the Jewish community that once existed in the town is maintained by a group of historians and philanthropists, both Jewish and non-Jewish alike, across the state and beyond. Through the efforts of groups like the ISJL and the Freyhan Foundation, the Jews of the bayou remain historically vital.

The museum of the West Feliciana Historical Society in Louisiana holds a small collection of historic items that relate to the Jewish community of the area. But the legacy of the Jewish communities along the delta is undoubtedly larger than physical remnants. In New Orleans, Tivoli Circle, where the first Temple Sinai once stood, is now Lee Circle, and in the center, a tall pillar supports a statue of Confederate General

New Orleans's old Gates of Prayer synagogue on Jackson Avenue and Chippewa Street, built in 1867. This synagogue has been neglected for years and is in need of rehabilitation. *Photograph by Emily Ford.*

Lee. Adjacent to the statute stands the thoroughly modern K&B Plaza Building—the only structure that still bears the emblem of the drugstore chain. The landscape across the Mississippi River delta region tells a story much greater than documents and histories, as evidenced by such buildings as the old Gates of Prayer synagogue in New Orleans. Over the past 250 years, New Orleans and the towns upriver from it have changed from frontier backwater communities to thriving commercial centers. Through the oil booms, the decline of the rural South and the replacement of steamboats with enormous tankers on their way to the Gulf of Mexico, the Jewish communities of the South have been indispensable players in the region's heritage, fueling the economic engines and tending the hearths of the homefront.

Bibliography

Adams, Maurianne, and John Bracey. *Strangers and Neighbors: Relations Between Blacks & Jews in the United States.* Amherst: University of Massachusetts Press, 1999.

Alexander, Daniel. *Congregation Gates of Prayer: 150 Years of Service to the Jewish Community.* Metairie, LA: Congregation Gates of Prayer, 2001.

American Jewish Committee, Jewish Publication Society of America. *American Jewish Yearbook.* Vol. 21. Philadelphia, PA: American Jewish Committee, 1919.

Arthur, Stanley. *Old New Orleans, A History of the Vieux Carré, Its Ancient and Historical Buildings.* Westminster, MD: Heritage Books, 1936.

Ashkenazi, Elliot. *The Business of Jews in Louisiana, 1840–1875.* Tuscaloosa: University of Alabama Press, 1988.

Barry, John. *Rising Tide: The Great Mississippi Flood of 1927 and How It Changed America.* New York: Simon & Schuster, 1998.

Bauman, Mark, and Berkley Kalin, eds. *The Quiet Voices: Southern Rabbis and Black Civil Rights, 1880s to 1990s.* Tuscaloosa: University of Alabama Press, 1997.

Bergquist, James. *Daily Life in Immigrant America, 1820–1870.* Westport, CT: Greenwood Press, 2008.

Bloch, Anny. "Mercy on Rude Streams: Jewish Emigrants from Alsace-Lorraine to the Lower Mississippi Region and the Concept of Fidelity." *Southern Jewish History*, 3 (1999): 81–110.

Brown, Yvonne. "Tolerance and Bigotry in Southwest Louisiana: The Ku Klux Klan, 1921–23." *Louisiana History: The Journal of the Louisiana Historical Association* 47, no. 2 (Spring 2006): 153–68.

Campanella, Catherine. *New Orleans City Park.* Charleston, SC: Arcadia Publishing, 2011.

Chafets, Zev. *Members of the Tribe.* N.p.: Random House Digital, 2011.

Christovich, Mary, ed. *New Orleans Architecture.* Vol. 3, *The Cemeteries.* Gretna, LA: Pelican Publishing, 2004.

Christovich, Mary, Roulhac Toledano and Betsy Swanson. *New Orleans Architecture.* Vol. 2, *The American Sector.* Gretna, LA: Pelican Publishing, 1998.

Cohen, Rich. *The Fish That Ate the Whale: The Life and Times of America's Banana King.* New York: Macmillan, 2012.

Conrad, Glenn, and Ray Lucas. *White Gold: A Brief History of the Louisiana Sugar Industry, 1795–1995.* Lafayette: University of Southwestern Louisiana Press, 1995.

Daily Picayune. "Death of Peter R. Middlemiss." September 13, 1887.

Davis, Edwin. *Louisiana: The Pelican State*. Baton Rouge: Louisiana State University Press, 1959.

Dawdy, Shannon. *Building the Devil's Empire: French Colonial New Orleans*. Chicago: University of Chicago Press, 2008.

Diner, Hasia, and Beryl Benderly. *Her Works Praise Her: A History of Jewish Women in America from Colonial Times to the Present*. New York: Basic Books, 2002.

Dinnerstein, Leonard, and Mary Palsson, eds. *Jews in the South*. Baton Rouge: Louisiana State University Press, 1976.

Dossman, Steven. *Marching Through Mississippi: Soldier and Civilian Action During the Vicksburg Campaign*. Ann Arbor: University of Michigan Press, 2008.

Epstien, John. *K&B Drug Stores*. Charleston, SC: Arcadia Publishing, 2011.

Evans, Eli. *The Provincials: A Personal History of Jews in the South*. New York: Simon & Schuster, 1997.

Feibelman, Julian. *A Social and Economic Study of the New Orleans Jewish Community*. Philadelphia, PA: Julian Feibelman, 1941.

Ferris, Marcie. *Matzo Ball Gumbo: Culinary Tales of the Jewish South*. Chapel Hill: University of North Carolina Press, 2005.

Ferris, Marcie, and Mark Greenberg. *Jewish Roots in Southern Soil: A New History*. Waltham, MA: Brandeis University Press, 2006.

Finkelstein, Norman. *American Jewish History*. Philadelphia, PA: Jewish Publication Society, 2007.

Fortier, Alcée. *A History of Louisiana*. Vol. 2. Paris, France: Goupil & Company, 1904.

Frank, Lisa. *Women in the American Civil War*. New York: ABC-CLIO, 2008.

Frank, Lisa, and Peter Mancall. *Civil War: People and Perspectives*. Santa Barbara, CA: ABC-CLIO, 2009.

Golden, Harry. *Our Southern Landsman*. New York: G.P. Putnam's Sons, 1974.

Goodspeed Publishing Company. *Biographical and Historical Sketches of Louisiana*. Chicago: Goodspeed Publishing Company, 1892.

Guice, John. "Bedfellows and Bedbugs: Stands on the Natchez Trace." *Southern Quarterly* 48, no. 1 (Fall 2010): 7–26.

Gurock, Jeffrey. *American Jewish History*. Vol. 3. New York: Taylor & Francis Publishing, 1998.

Heller, Max. *Jubilee Souvenir of Temple Sinai, 1872–1922*. New Orleans: American Printing, 1922.

Herscovici, Julius. *The Jews of Vicksburg, Mississippi*. Philadelphia, PA: Xlibris, 2007.

Hoffman, Kenneth. "The Small-Town Southern Jewish Experience: Port Gibson, Mississippi, A Case Study." MA thesis, Tulane University, 1993.

Holmes, William. "Whitecapping: Anti-Semitism in the Populist Era." *American Jewish Historical Quarterly* 63, no. 3 (1974): 244–61.

James, Clayton. *Antebellum Natchez*. Baton Rouge: Louisiana State University Press, 1968.

Kaganoff, Nathan, and Melvin Urofsky, eds. *Turn to the South: Essays on Southern Jewry*. Charlottesville: University Press of Virginia, 1979.

Korn, Bertram. *The Early Jews of New Orleans*. Waltham, MA: American Jewish Historical Society, 1969.

———. *Jews and Negro Slavery in the Old South 1789–1865*. Elkins Park, PA: Reform Congregation Keneseth Israel, 1961.

Laborde, Peggy, and John Magill. *Canal Street: New Orleans' Great Wide Way*. Gretna, LA: Pelican Publishing Company, 2006.

Langley, Lester, and Thomas Schooner. *The Banana Men: American Mercenaries and Entrepreneurs in Central America, 1880–1930*. Lexington: University Press of Kentucky, 1995.

Malone, Bobbie. "New Orleans Uptown Jewish Immigrants: The Community of Congregation Gates of Prayer." *Louisiana History: The Journal of the Louisiana Historical Association* 32, no. 3 (Summer 1991): 239–87.

———. *Rabbi Max Heller: Reformer, Zionist, Southerner, 1860–1929*. Tuscaloosa: University of Alabama Press, 1997.

Marcus, Jacob, ed. *Memoirs of American Jew 1775–1865*. Vols. 1–3. Philadelphia, PA: Jewish Publication Society of America, 1955.

Markham, Jerry W. *A Financial History of the United States*. Vols. 1 and 2. North Castle, NY: M.E. Sharpe Publishing, 2002.

McLemore, Richard, ed. *A History of Mississippi*. Vol. I. Hattiesburg: University & College Press of Mississippi, 1973.

Meade, Robert. *Judah P. Benjamin: Confederate Statesman*. New York: Arno Press, 1975.

Menken, Stanwood. *Hebrew Sheltering and Immigrant Society of America, Report on the formation of the first Russian Jewish colony in the United States at Catahoula Parish, Louisiana*. N.p.: Stephens, Hayter & Co., 1882.

Meyers, Rose. *A History of Baton Rouge 1699–1812*. Baton Rouge: Louisiana State University Press, 1976.

New Orleans Magazine. "New Orleans at the Time of Comus." January 2007. http://www.myneworleans.com/New-Orleans-Magazine/January-2007.

Phillippsborn, Gertrude. *The History of the Jewish Community of Vicksburg, from 1820–1968*. Vicksburg, MS: 1969.

Pope, John. "Leon Godchaux II, Sugar and Department-store Businessman, Dies at 94." *New Orleans Times-Picayune*, September 20, 2011.

Powell, Lawrence. "When Hate Came to Town: New Orleans' Jews and George Lincoln Rockwell." *American Jewish History* 85, no. 4 (1997): 393–419.

Raphael, Marc, ed. *The Columbia History of Jews and Judaism in America*. New York: Columbia University Press, 2008.

Rightor, Henry, ed. *Standard History of New Orleans, Louisiana*. Chicago: Lewish Publishing Company, 1900.

Rockoff, Stuart. "The Mysterious Death of Marx Schoenburg." Goldring-Woldenburg Institute for Southern Jewish Life. (n.d.) Accessed June 2, 2012. http://www.isjl.org/history/archive/la/documents/TheMysteriousDeathofMarxSchoenberg.pdf.

Rosen, Robert. *The Jewish Confederates*. Columbia: University of South Carolina Press, 2000.

Sandlin, Lee. *Wicked River: The Mississippi When It Last Ran Wild*. New York: Pantheon Books, 2010.

Sarna, Jonathan. *American Judaism: A History*. New Haven, CT: Yale University Press, 2004.

Sarna, Jonathan, and Adam Mendelsohn. *Jews and the Civil War: A Reader*. New York: NYU Press, 2010.

Schmidt, Shra. "The Mehitza That Made Waves in New Orleans." *Jerusalem Post*, September 29, 2005.

Sentilles, Renée. *Performing Menken: Adah Isaacs Menken and the Birth of American Celebrity*. New York: Cambridge University Press, 2003.

Starr, Frederick, Robert Brantley and Jan Brantley. *Southern Comfort: The Garden District of New Orleans*. New York: Princeton Architectural Press, 1998.

Sternberg, Hans, and James Shallady. *We Were Merchants: The Sternberg Family and the Story of Goudchaux's and Maison Blanche Department Stores*. Baton Rouge: Louisiana State University Press, 2009.

Sussman, Lance. *Isaac Leeser and the Making of American Judaism*. Detroit, MI: Wayne State University Press, 1996.

Times Picayune. "Godchaux's Unusual History Dates Back to Youth with Pack." March 1, 1940.

Turitz, Leo, and Evelyn Turitz. *Jews in Early Mississippi*. Jackson: University Press of Mississippi, 1995.

United States Naval War Records Office. *Official Records of the Union and Confederate Navies in the War of the Rebellion*. Washington, D.C.: Government Printing Office, 1903.

Wall, Bennett, ed. *Louisiana: A History*. Wheeling, IL: Harlan Davidson, 2008.

Watson, Charles. *The History of Southern Drama*. Lexington: University Press of Kentucky, 1997.

Weissbach, Lee. "East European Immigrants and the Image of Jews in the Small-town South." *American Jewish History* (September 1997): 39–43.

———. *Jewish Life in Small-town America: A History*. New Haven, CT: Yale University Press, 2005.

White, Richard. *Kingfish: The Reign of Huey Long*. N.p.: Random House Digital, 2006.

Whitten, David, and Andrew Durnford. *A Black Sugar Planter in the Antebellum South*. New Brunswick, NJ: Transaction Publishers, 1995.

Wilds, John, Charles Dufour and Walter Cowan. *Louisiana Yesterday and Today: A Historical Guide to the State*. Baton Rouge: Louisiana State University Press, 1996.

Wilhelm, Cornelia. *The Independent Orders of B'nai B'rith and True Sisters: Pioneers of a New Jewish Identity, 1843–1914*. Detroit, MI: Wayne State University Press, 2011.

Wilkie, Laura. *Creating Freedom: Material Culture and African American Identity at Oakley Plantation, Louisiana, 1840–1950*. Baton Rouge: Louisiana State University Press, 2000.

Index

About the Authors

Emily Ford is a master's degree candidate in the College of Charleston/Clemson University Graduate Historic Preservation Program. She received her BA in history from the University of Florida in 2006. Ford has been involved in preservation efforts in and around New Orleans for a number of years, focusing primarily on cemetery preservation and archival research. Most recently, she has been instrumental in a documentation and restoration project for New Orleans's Lafayette Cemetery Number 1 with Save Our Cemeteries. This effort will contribute to her graduate thesis, which studies preservation issues specific to the New Orleans area. *The Jews of New Orleans and the Mississippi Delta* is her first published work.

Barry Stiefel is an assistant professor in the College of Charleston/Clemson University Graduate Historic Preservation Program. In 2008, Stiefel received his PhD in historic preservation from Tulane University in New Orleans. His research interests relate to the preservation of Jewish heritage with past research projects covering the synagogues of New Orleans and the Mississippi River delta area, as well as cultural connections between Louisiana's Jews with those in Alsace and Lorraine, France, and Quebec, Canada.

Visit us at
www.historypress.net

www.ingramcontent.com/pod-product-compliance
Lightning Source LLC
Chambersburg PA
CBHW070355100426
42812CB00005B/1518